MW00605545

HOW TO MANAGE
SELF-STORAGE

THE KEY TO $UCCESS

TOM LITTON

Copyright © 2009 Tom Litton. All rights reserved.

Published by MiniCo, Inc., Phoenix, Arizona

No part of this publication may be reproduced, stored in a retrieval system, or transmitted in any form or by any means, electronic, mechanical, photocopying, recording, scanning, or otherwise, except as permitted under Section 107 or 108 of the 1976 United States Copyright Act, without prior written expression of the Publisher. Requests to the Publisher for permission should be addressed to MiniCo Publishing Division, 2531 W. Dunlap Ave., Phoenix, AZ 85021, (602) 870-1711, fax (602) 678-3511.

Limit of Liability/Disclaimer of Warranty: While the publisher and authors have used their best efforts in preparing this book, they make no representations or warranties with respect to the accuracy or completeness of the contents of this book and specifically disclaim any implied warranties of merchantability or fitness for a particular purpose. No warranty may be created or extended by sales representatives or written sales materials. The advice and strategies contained herein may not be suitable for your situation. You should consult with a professional where appropriate. Neither the publisher nor the author shall be liable for any loss of profit or any other commercial damages, including but not limited to special, incidental, consequential, or other damages.

0-9771578-4-9

Cover Design by Jeffry Pettingill

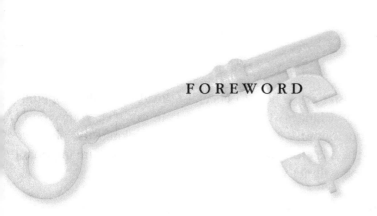

FOREWORD

Tom's done it again. "A book on storage management?" I queried. Yeah, right.

All of us have been taught. All of us have been managed. We all know when teaching is good or fun. We can tell in a heartbeat if management is bad. It reflects in morale. Some of us can tell when management is good. Usually it's good, or even great, when we aren't noticing. The thing is, many people think that just because they've been on the receiving end of these critical skills that they innately know how to teach, how to manage. Sadly, that's just not the case.

Sometimes, with some nudging or some reflection, the untrained can step up to the plate and show others the way. Because that's the crux of management, isn't it? To show others the way things need to be done? To set policy on a rational basis and then to implement it? Management is half psychology, half results oriented, and half learning to avoid the thin spots in the ice. But that's more than two halves, right? That's the problem of management; it's learning to juggle when people just keep adding extra balls.

This book won't make you an instant manager of people. I doubt there's a program out there that can. But this book will help you to order your own thinking in a way that lets good management out of the box. It's a start. It's the beginning of looking at the skeleton of your organizational framework so that you can flesh it out with the kind of management that fits your style, your organization, your facility.

Written in a way that's fun, accessible, and tailored to the storage environment, this book reaches into your common sense to give you a starting place for finding your storage management chops. Tom's voice is always present in that "little voice in the back of your head" way, to keep you on track, to keep you honest. It isn't just a how-to checklist. Read correctly (hopefully at least once a year), it ignites your internal debate on what your type of management is about, because we need to have you thinking. Too often we reduce things to a checklist format and forget why these items are important to check. Tom's book will get you thinking.

I don't agree with everything in this book—it's part of being a lawyer. The minute things start looking simple, I come up with the exceptions. While that makes me great fun at a party, it doesn't make me qualified to write a book on management. Sometimes too much information ... well, you know. Tom seems to have distilled this down to just the right mix: practical and applicable. Just when I want to raise my hand and yell "But!" I see the simple wisdom in his approach. He doesn't address every question, but he does address enough questions that perhaps you'll start filling in the blanks with your own answers. If something in it pushes your buttons, I suggest you can look at that too.

So, go ahead. Take this mental agility test and see if it changes the way you think about managing people, and maintenance, and administration, and training, and, and , and ... well, you get it, that's what management is all about!

Alta V. Walters
Attorney At Law

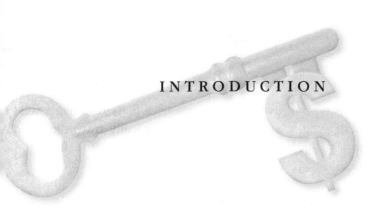

The Art Of Self-Storage Management

Managing people is an art form. While we tend to view management as controlling people to get work done, the reality is that management is the ability to lead, coach, and inspire others to work purposefully towards achieving common goals.

So what is management? For self-storage owners and operators, it means managing our managers. Thus, one's role as manager—and more importantly as a leader—is vital in making self-storage management viable. Self-storage is unique in that as operators, we typically manage older employees who have a wealth of life experiences, values, and wounds. Managing these self-storage managers involves earning their respect and encouraging them to balance daily details with relentless customer service, all while keeping a smile on their face and a spring in their step. As such, managing is a difficult challenge to say the least.

Michael Vance, one time trainer for the Disney Corporation, once provided this unusual definition of leadership:

"Leadership is the ability to establish and manage a creative climate where members of the organization are self-motivated towards the mastery of long range constructive goals that are compatible with their personal values."

In other words, management is the ability to inspire vision, while at the same time balancing the objectives of the organization. The reality is that self-storage management, especially for self-storage managers, can be boring and in many ways, unrewarding. For the most part, a typical storage manager's day is very similar to the movie "Groundhog Day" starring Bill Murray. Each day in the life of a self-storage manager is essentially the same as the day before. This type of dynamic necessitates a leader/manager who understands that managing self-storage is not intrinsically rewarding and must motivate, support, and inspire self-storage managers in oftentimes unusual and creative ways.

Current Self-Storage Management Styles

Before discussing management styles, we should begin with a discussion of the nature of a self-storage manager's job. Self-storage managers are the front line contacts with our customers. Moreover, they are often the only contact person with our customers. In other words, they truly carry the face of the organization from day of rental to day of termination. In many respects, their jobs are very difficult because they must wear many different hats and excel in many different roles. Every individual tends to develop a management style, typically resultant of the way they were managed as a young adult or a style that is merely an extension of their own personal belief system and communications style. There are several predominant management styles in self-storage management, they are:

- Supervisory
- Managerial
- Leadership
- Hands-off, manager-driven

Supervisory—These supervisors have a tendency to "over supervise and under manage." Most managers resent being over supervised. This is due in large part to the fact that as an industry, we tend to hire older employees. Older employees have a rich history of life experiences and have often labored under horrendous supervisors in the past. One of the most common self-storage manager complaints is that they are treated as property "babysitters." Self-storage managers do not need supervision, they need direction. The "supervisory style" is very common among larger management companies that hire younger college graduates who have an educational background but lack real life work experience. The supervisory style works well in manufacturing, construction, and other blue collar industries, however, in self-storage it is usually counterproductive.

RH role

Managerial—The typical "managerial style" usually involves an individual or individuals anointed with responsibility for several properties. Most companies refer to these individuals as "property manager," a simple, mid-level management person. Most experienced property managers have a span of control of three to 10 facilities and can easily oversee their properties if they avail themselves of current technology such as e-mail, cell phones, outsourced shopping services, etc. Property managers usually have college degrees or have demonstrated proven skills by first working at self-storage facilities as facility managers and have the ability to relate well to others.

Property managers must command the respect of the managers they lead. Most managers do not respect their property manager until they demonstrate on-site job skills. Many astute self-storage owners who grow to the point where they need a mid-level management person will require that the trainee work at a self-storage facility for a few months until they gain the necessary counter skills. While college degrees more than prepare an individual academically for self-storage management, self-storage is a unique business environment where real world work experience is necessary to understand the dynamics of the job and the rigors as well.

Most property managers/owners fail to visit the property with a specific agenda. This book contains a chapter devoted to the concept that "what gets measured, gets done." Effective managers will always prepare for property visits, solicit feedback, and document their discussions. The managerial style tends to focus on relationships first rather than didactic skills, therefore, it is wise to keep the property visit focused by using a specific agenda. Once the agenda items are discussed, then the manager can develop and foster relationships.

Good property managers/owners are good teachers, coaches, and mentors. The managerial style recognizes the power of coaching and teaching rather than supervising. While effective managers are obviously both male and female, it seems as though females fulfill this role particularly well. This is due in large part to their attention to detail, coupled with the ability to empathize with tenants. Look for candidates, male and female, who demonstrate these skills and talents.

Lastly, once again, good property managers/owners need to invest "apron time." Effective property managers know the details of the job or are at least able to quickly learn the business. Managers are reluctant to follow property manager direction if they suspect that they do not know or understand the business.

Leadership—The leadership style is usually seen in very large companies or occasionally small owners who lead their employees rather than manage or supervise them. Leaders determine direction, but they do not necessarily row the oars. Tom Smith of Auburn, Calif., is an example of the quintessential "leadership" style leader. Tom owns and operates several self-storage facilities in Northern California. Tom allows his managers to manage their properties with little direct supervision or involvement. Rather, Tom monitors the numbers, visits the facility, and encourages the managers. As a result, Tom tends to attract self-motivated, self-starting managers who do not need supervision or management. Like Tom, disciplined leaders learn to live by the numbers. Leaders know that managers don't care how much you know until they know how much you care. Leaders must make the tough decisions. Leaders teach and live company values and philosophy. In order to use this leadership style, the leader must invest a great deal of time in finding the right managers with the right view of storage operations management. In order to be a leader rather than a manager, the leader must hire and inspire self-motivated, self-regulating, and self-starting managers. Unfortunately, this type of manager is not easy to find; obtaining one requires much diligence.

Hands-off, Manager-Driven—Many self-storage owners tend to hire managers and simply turn the business over to them. This is typically the result of a lack of knowledge about daily operations. This management style tends to predominate with the small self-storage facility owner/operator. Many owners assume that the managers have the same objectives and simply know more about the daily operations of the business than they do. Regrettably, this management style leads to many of the unfortunate lawsuits seen in our industry like lawsuits that involve disgruntled employees or tenants who sue for wrongful sale, theft, or injury. The hands-off, manager-driven style is wrought with many pitfalls and is usually the result of a self-storage owner who sees the facility as a "passive investment" rather than the business entity that it is.

Give a person a fish and you feed them for a day; teach them to fish and you feed them for life. Managers and leaders will take the time to teach every employee the business and how they think. Supervisors tend to dictate rather than explain the background behind policies or why they are important.

Good managers need little supervision or management; however, we all need leadership! Most self-storage managers crave leadership and will follow a leader much easier than a supervisor or even a property manager. Property managers can become very effective leaders if they adopt the role of coach, mentor, and supporter.

Do not allow the facility to become "manager driven." The number one axiom for the study of economics is "everyone acts in their own self-interest." Even Michael Jordan had a coach. We all need leadership, supervision, management, or coaching. Everyone will act in their own self-interest if left unchecked. Leaders, supervisors, and managers understand this simple fact about human nature and account for it.

Remember that 80 percent of your problems stem from 20 percent of your managers. The most unappreciated segment of our society is made up of the achievers and producers. Don't forget to continually challenge and fight this tendency to forget about what is going well by only focusing on what is going wrong. Many young parents make this simple mistake; they focus on the misbehavior rather than compliance. Effective leaders, managers, and supervisors all agree that you tend to get more of what you reward!

Simple Ways To Sharpen Your Managerial Style

- **Share your financials.** Managers are often surprised to learn that the dollars that they deposit are not net profits. Many managers simply do not know how much it costs to operate a business. Share your financial statements with them and challenge them to keep costs down.

- **Ask them for marketing plans.** When you plan for marketing, it tends to get done because it has become a priority and it has been committed to writing. This book addresses marketing plans and just how effective they can be. Remember, "What gets measured, gets done!"

- **Conduct "red flag" meetings every month.** Red flag meetings are simply meetings designed to formally review the performance of the facility. The meeting is designed to involve all pertinent parties so that every team member knows whether the business is operating well and what commitments need to be made. This book will address red flag meetings in a later chapter.

- **Hold them accountable for results.** Most managers are liberated when they are held accountable for results. Employees report much greater satisfaction when they can evaluate their own performance and determine whether they are performing satisfactorily. Most self-storage owners never share the performance results with their managers unless they are unhappy with it!

- **Give them decision-making authority.** Supervisors tend to hoard the decision-making authority, thereby making the managers feel inferior and untrustworthy. The reality is that if you cannot trust a managers' decision-making authority, they should not be on the payroll. While decision-making authority has its limits, good leaders or managers give as much decision authority as possible to their managers.

- **Pay them for superior performance.** Pay tends to be the great reward. While most employees rank pay as second or third on their list of job satisfaction criteria, rewards, especially monetary, become the yardstick of success. For example, Warren Buffet clearly doesn't work diligently every day because he needs more money; he needs and thrives on success and recognition. When managers perform well, you should reward them.

- **Teach them the owner's mind set.** When you teach another person to think like you do, you teach them how to make the same or similar decisions that you would make given the same fact pattern. This is liberating for both parties. The leader/manager does not always have to carry the burden of daily decision making and the manager feels more and more competent each time a correct decision is made. Effective leaders/managers teach their managers that it is better to "ask for forgiveness than to ask for permission." While this saying seems bold, it encourages the manager to exercise independent thinking and responsibility. Leaders/managers are not afraid to relinquish decision-making power as it better serves the organization and frees the leader/manager for more productive pursuits.

CHAPTER ONE

Hiring And Firing Facility Managers

Hiring and firing are two of the most important tasks of the manager/ owner, the person who has to get results through others. The first is complex and difficult; the second is stressful and difficult. Both sets of skills must be learned through study and experience if the manager/ owner is to be successful.

A key element in being successful in self-storage is your ability to recruit, hire, and build a team of competent and effective people. Therefore, the ability to select good managers is critical to the success of any facility and to your success as a manager/owner.

Because people management is more of an art form than an academic discipline, you cannot be transformed by simply reading a book. The reality is that even with the very best hiring skills, your success rate will only be about 66 percent. One-third of the people you hire will probably not work out. This does not reflect any particular weakness on your part, but is rather the complex and oftentimes unusual interworkings of the human mind.

Hiring competent and motivated managers is the most important aspect of self-storage management.

Hiring the right people absolutely determines your success or failure in self-storage. Hiring the right people will liberate you and make your life easy. Hiring the wrong people will destroy your success and probably give you a heart attack!

The Selection Process
The selection process is the key to your success and the success of your facilities. Remember: The first law of self-storage management is selection.

Three Things To Remember When Hiring

1. Even if you are great at hiring people, you will only be right 66 percent of the time.

2. The most common mistake made by managers/owners is to rush the hiring decision. Take your time!

3. The number one fear of most managers/owners is that they cannot run the facility in the event the manager quits.

Ninety-five percent of your success is your ability to choose the right people to manage the facility.

It is also important to remember that hiring is an art and is forged through experience and mistakes. The process cannot be rushed. To be effective, you must take your time in hiring self-storage managers. Unfortunately, rushing is the most common hiring mistake made in self-storage management. Moreover, hiring the wrong person is the most expensive mistake you can make. Here's why.

First, customers are leery of manager turnover. Poor managers can quickly damage all your customer goodwill. Remember that 12 percent of your new rentals are referrals from existing customers who are hopefully happy with you. Another 12 percent of your customers are repeat customers who have rented in the past. Second, all of your training costs are wasted if you make a poor hiring decision. Training can be time consuming and costly. Facilities almost always suffer economically during a training period. Moreover, poor hiring decisions can result in legal costs and court judgments and can be mentally and physically taxing on any manager/owner. In today's litigious society, hiring the wrong resident manager team can literally break you. Remember that your insurance coverage does not protect you from employee-related litigation.

It is important to note that in self-storage management, the natural tendency is to hire a manager as a solution to a pressing problem. The most common pressing problem is that the facility is without a manager and the assistant is managing the facility.

Matching The Employee To The Job

What do we really want from a self-storage manager/employee? What are the outputs we expect? Do you explain your expectations to your managers? Is there a clear benchmark so that the manager can self-evaluate their performance? Do you effectively track the results you are getting and convey this information to your employees?

It is important to think about all of these things before hiring. The effective self-storage manager/owner has clearly defined performance standards that are reviewed every month. It is also important to know up front what ideal skills you expect in a self-storage manager candidate. Here are some of the key critical areas.

Self-storage managers must have the ability to interact with others. The manager must be a "people person" who enjoys frequent contact, of a short duration, with the general public from all walks of life. If a prospective candidate cannot impress you in an interview, they will not impress your potential customers. Do not hire "wall flowers" to work in your facility and then become angry at their inability to relate to others!

The manager should be outgoing and friendly. When hiring teams, generally only one member of the team fits this profile. Effective managers must "naturally" enjoy public contact and actually thrive on it. Properties don't compete, their managers do! When customers are polled, the overwhelming majority cite "the manager was nice to me" as their primary reason for storing and staying once they have stored. In addition, the manager must enjoy serving the needs of others. If you want a customer service oriented manager, you must hire one.

In today's world, self-storage managers must be goal-oriented self-starters. They must work independently with little or no supervision. This is important to remember because some employees cannot work well in this type of environment. If you tend to hire employees who need constant supervision, you must adjust your management style accordingly.

Storage managers must use discretion before acting. This characteristic is called "judgment" and is important in self-storage management. Managers must also possess good "follow-through" skills. Generally, with a team, only one team member needs this skill. Follow-through skills are important as self-storage management is heavily dependent on these skills. In other words, do not hire a manager who has poor follow-through skills because they will simply be miserable in the job.

Adaptability is also essential for self-storage managers. This is a key attribute for which to look; after all, customer service is dependent on an open mind and flexibility. While enforcing policies and rules is very important, successful managers tend to be very adaptive.

Storage managers cannot fear confrontation. A large part of their job is direct confrontation that must be tempered with customer service. While most adults avoid confrontation, the successful manager will approach confrontation by using their relationship skills rather than their perceived authority.

Communication is another key factor. Storage managers must be able to communicate well, both in person and in writing. Moreover, they should be open and expressive with their viewpoints and willing to share them with others. They must be frank, sincere, diplomatic, and tactful. A good indicator of this trait is a good sense of humor.

Look for a manager who is self-confident. In addition to being confident in their abilities, storage managers should be motivated by pride and a sense of accomplishment. A good indicator of this is in the resume. Look for statements proclaiming past accomplishments.

Storage managers should be able to accept input regarding their shortcomings and have the capability of accepting suggestions. They cannot take criticism too personally, whether it is from customers or the property managers/owners. Remember: Managers who are "perfectionists" are more prone to taking criticism personally and internalizing their feelings. Consequently, managing the perfectionist can be very draining, both to the owner/property manager and the public at large.

It is also essential for self-storage managers to have certain thinking patterns. In addition to being reasonably intelligent, they must have problem solving, computer, and math skills. They must be able to work in a purposeful, deliberate manner and organize their own responsibilities. Applicants who have never worked in an independent environment may not like the lack of direct supervision that self-storage requires. For self-starting, self-motivated applicants, self-storage is the perfect job description.

Enthusiasm and innovation skills are great to possess, however they are not always good indicators of a superior self-storage manager. While the enthusiastic, innovative applicant may be tempting, they typically represent the consummate salesman and may not have the right blend of job skills needed for storage management. Also, remember that storage managers tend to think the same way they look, act, and dress. If you are a fanatic about cleanliness, don't hire someone who struggles with cleanliness and order.

Here is another question that should be addressed up front: Can the opening you have be filled by a single person rather than a team? In many instances, a single person with an assistant and a good maintenance person can manage a facility better than a team. Analyze your work requirements and ask yourself if a team approach is really warranted. The self-storage industry has actually slowly moved away from management teams as a staffing approach. This is due in large part to the difficulty in finding suitable management teams.

The Job Description
While job descriptions are important, most new job candidates simply do not know enough about our business to know whether or not they will enjoy the job. You can present the job candidate with a job description that details your overall expectations. For experienced managers, you can present both your job description and performance standards and gauge their response and receptivity. When designing job descriptions, think about the following:

- What is the manager expected to do?
- List every function and responsibility.
- Evaluate to whom the manager will be reporting.
- Decide what type of attitude or personality the successful manager must possess.

Think about the successful self-storage managers you have hired or met and determine what made them successful and why. Ask yourself what the most important attribute is for your position and hire for that attribute. Remember, you will never find a manager who is stellar at everything. Most contemporary property managers/owners look for sales and marketing oriented managers. Therefore, match the personality of the manager to the personality of the facility.

Finding Good Candidates

One of the most important aspects of finding good managers is to find good candidates. Most self-storage property managers/owners say this has become virtually impossible. While there are no special secrets to finding good candidates, there are common techniques.

Your own existing employees are a good source of potential job candidates. We have a tendency to associate with like minded and like talented individuals. Really good, solid performing managers tend to know other, really good, potentially good managers. This is often overlooked when searching for suitable candidates. Offer a "bounty" if a manager refers anyone who is eventually hired by the company. While a bounty of $500 to $1,500 sounds expensive, the reality is that a good hire is well worth this much—if not more! Also, allow managers who have performed well to relocate to other properties. Self-storage managers often need new challenges. Good self-storage managers will work hard and need the new stimulation. If you have multiple locations, this is a great managerial strategy by allowing good performers the ability to relocate.

Your own personal contacts may be a good source for job candidates. Personal contacts must be cultivated all the time. Visit storage facilities as a hobby. Keep the business cards of managers who impressed you. Another strategy is to write your name on the back of your business card and tell an impressive manager that if they ever need a job or know of a good candidate who may need a job to call you in the future. If you receive a call from a manager who says that you gave them your business card, then you will know that they were a managerial candidate who impressed you. Always have someone who you want to hire someday. If nothing else, you will always see a good or bad idea that you can use. Above all, never ever hire family members!

Placement agencies, as a general rule, are fair sources of self-storage manager candidates. The best placement agency is the one that specializes in self-storage; however, these placement agencies tend to be short lived.

Newspaper ads tend to be the poorest way to find facility managers if you are looking for a management team; however, if you are looking for an individual manager, newspaper advertisements work very well. Here are some tips regarding newspaper ads:

- Only advertise on weekends.
- Resolve yourself to the fact that many unqualified applicants will call or send resumes.
- Advertise in the "Retail" section of the employment ads. Since retail has become a vital component of self-storage operations, it stands to reason that retail employees are a good fit.

Job Web sites can be another good source for finding managers. Advertise on Web sites such as craigslist.org, monster.com, careerbuilder.com, local job sites, etc. There are literally hundreds, if not thousands, of career-oriented Web sites that offer job listings and placement. When describing your job, use retail language in the advertisement to attract retail experienced applicants.

Do not use the words "self-storage" in your advertisement. There seems to be a stigma associated with self-storage. The best strategy is to explain the nature of the job to applicants after receiving their resumes or other contact information. Most retail applicants are surprised to learn that self-storage pays better than retail positions.

Also, ask applicants to e-mail or fax their resumes to you and provide a temporary e-mail address. When you receive their information, pay close attention to their adherence to your instructions on how to respond to the job listing. Their attention to detail, response time, and professionalism is very telling when evaluating them for your position.

The Art Of Interviewing
The best way to interview is to be prepared. A common mistake is to interview without a plan. To be effective, you must plan your interview; do not rely on just your "gut instinct," and apply the same framework for all candidates. Your interviewing style will be based on your own personal preferences, however here are some valuable tips:

- Write out and follow a written interview format.
- Take copious notes.
- Know your questions in advance.
- Always explain to the candidate that this is just an "exploratory interview."

Your initial interview should only last about 30 minutes. Clearly explain what you mean by "exploratory." In other words, explain that it is important to determine if there is a fit between the company and the candidate. Also explain that if the interviewer does not feel as though there is a fit, the candidate will be told during the exploratory interview. This releases the awkwardness of saying that "I'll get back to you" or some other patronizing phrase. For example, explain by saying:

"This is an exploratory interview. You are evaluating us and our position as we are evaluating you and your desire and skills. I will explain our position and you may or may not be interested. Our goal is to match what we know about the job with the right person so that the employee will be successful in the position. If after hearing about the position you do not see a fit, it is perfectly acceptable to simply say that you do not see a good fit. Conversely, if we don't see a good fit, I will tell you. Our goal here is not to impress each other, but rather to see if a mutually beneficial relationship can be forged."

During the exploratory interview, start out by explaining the overall job description including the basic compensation and benefits package. It is a good idea to explain what self-storage managers like about the job and those areas they typically do not like. Also, let the applicant know that your objective is to match the person to the job, not the job to the person.

Ask the prospective candidate if they see a fit between what the company is looking for and their job skills, motivations, and career goals. Emphasize that a proper fit is more important than both parties being disenchanted with the relationship after employment has begun. Very few companies approach the hiring decision this way. The traditional approach is that the prospective employer does most of the talking while the prospective employee feigns interest, tries to secure the position, and immediately begins looking for a better job once he or she receives their first paycheck. If a fit is not evident, simply tell the applicant right then.

When interviewing, look for past achievements, awards, or indicators of past job-related results. People who are successful tend to continue to be successful. If the last success story to which they can relate is 10 years old, think twice. Tell the applicant that you expect a hard working team. Use "what if" or hypothetical questions and situations to gauge their propensity toward hard work.

The initial interview is like the first date—if the candidate makes no attempt to impress you, they probably never will. A good job candidate will ask good, intelligent questions. Remember that they must enjoy the job as well. If a candidate does not ask questions, they may be desperate to accept any position.

If you are interviewing experienced self-storage managers, it is a good idea to ask about their opinions on the following:

- Anniversary versus first-of-the-month due dates
- Deposits versus administrative fees
- Delinquent customers and policies
- Customer conveniences and/or services
- After-hours "interruptions" by customers
- Their experience regarding income and occupancy growth

Don't engage in a debate; simply ask them about their opinion. What you are looking for in their response to these questions is not what their opinions really are, but rather their passion in talking about them. Look for a results orientation, flexibility, and a pro-customer service attitude.

Always interview a potential job candidate at least three times. Anyone can impress you once, but it takes a genuine individual or team to impress you three or more times. We have all learned this while dating. Once a couple has dated two or three times, both parties begin to see things in their potential partners. The same holds true for job candidates. Additionally, always try to interview potential job applicants in three different places.

Tips For Interviewing Potential Managers

- Trust your instinct or "gut." It is more accurate than you might think.

- Always have a potential job applicant interviewed, at least once, by a woman. You should get a perspective from both genders. Women tend to be better judges of character. The reason that women are better at interviewing is because they trust their instincts.

- Always have your most experienced and least experienced managers interview your candidates and listen to their input. Those areas that your best and worst managers see in potential job applicants are really telling. Do not defend or embellish the applicants in any way; always solicit input on prospective candidates from several sources and ask those sources to be very candid. Be sure to make notations.

Look At Past Performance
Past performance is almost always an indicator of future success. People who succeed become accustomed to succeeding. People who do not succeed generally repeat their errors. Therefore, ask questions about previous successes. Ask the applicant about their "greatest achievement." If an applicant hesitates about achievements, it may be due to the fact that they haven't experienced any lately.

Ask the applicant what past experiences they possess that will enable them to succeed in your position, and hire on proven past performance only. Ask for specific details about past performances. A high achiever will always quote specific numbers, percentages, etc. Listen for pride and a sense of accomplishment in their voice.

Try to determine if an experienced manager has 10 years of experience or simply one year's experience 10 times. Do not necessarily shy away from someone who has worked for several previous owners. Oftentimes, good managers work hard, are not justly compensated, and simply move on. The old stigma of job hopping no longer applies. In today's economy, job hopping simply implies that the candidate has "richness of experience."

Résumés And References
Résumés tend to be poor indicators of future success as they tend to only accent the positive and tend to be informational only. Let's discuss some ideas on résumés and references.

Résumés should be simple, honest, and should focus on accomplishments and achievements. Also, look for typographical errors and inconsistencies. The reality is that the résumé tells very little, but it is a starting place. Remember, however, that in general, references can be practically worthless, especially give that in today's legal climate, most people are reluctant to offer much information, much less be candid about problem employees. Nevertheless, it is important to check on an employee's references; if asked the right questions, they can be a good source of information. Reference sources tend to be honest if asked the right questions.

Making The Right Decision
The actual decision to hire is yours. Your entire success as a property manager or owner rests with your ability to hire the right person. Everyone has their own style and set of criteria. Here are some questions to ask yourself about your new hire:

- Does this person or team's personality match the personality of the facility?
- Would you enjoy spending a week with this person if you were stranded on a desert island?

Tips For Calling On References

- Telephone the reference personally. Don't delegate this important step. You need to hear their responses with your own ears.

- Ask the reference about the candidate's strengths and weaknesses. Most references will tend to only talk positively about an ex-employee. The best way to draw them out is to simply say "In fairness, I know that everyone has strengths and weaknesses, what do you think this ex-employee's weaknesses are?" If the reference states that there are no weaknesses, then you know that their information is tainted.

- If you are calling a previous employer, ask to speak with someone who worked for or with the candidate. This can be very revealing! Oftentimes, just the suspicious way in which a company will not speak with you can be telling.

- Always ask this question: "Is there anything else that I should know?" Any psychologist or counselor will tell you that the most significant part of any conversation is the last 20 percent of what is said.

- If you owned the facility, would you hire this person to work for you?
- Would you let your mother fly with this person if they were the pilot?
- Would you leave the country for a year and entrust your facility to this person, knowing that you cannot exercise any authority over the facility until you return?

Remember: It is important to be "slow to hire, and quick to fire."

When An Employee Doesn't Work Out
There are four problems indigenous to self-storage management that you cannot control or cure. The first is an employee or team who has lost their motivation. The burnout period for resident managers tends to be about two

to three years, with burnout experienced sooner at facilities in "economically-challenged" neighborhoods.

Burnout is less problematic, however, with individual managers who do not reside on the premises; nevertheless, burnout does occur to virtually all managers at some point.

The second situation is whereby the employee or team is simply not competent to perform the job or some critical component of it—this is actually rare in self-storage. The third scenario is when the employee steals from the company. Theft cannot be tolerated and must be dealt with quickly.

The last situation, and far more grim, occurs when the employee or one member of the team passes away. Once a member of the team passes away, the balance of talents no longer meets the objectives of the facility. Remember, they were hired as a team.

In these four cases, the best strategy is to deal with the problem quickly. Each situation has unique problems and you should consult your legal counsel before proceeding.

Terminating an employee can be the most difficult part of daily self-storage management. You have finally decided that a change is necessary and the employee must be discharged. Firing has many legal ramifications that should be considered, and resident managers are perhaps the most difficult employees to terminate. Not only are they losing their jobs, but their home as well. Let's look at some suggestions for the firing process.

Always prepare your case. In other words, clearly document why you are terminating an employee. Be sure to collect documentation to support your firing decision. Rehearse the firing discussion in your mind. Practice on your spouse. Make notes to assist you during the initial remarks. Also, prepare a severance package in advance and be generous. This assumes that you have decided to terminate the manager simply because a fit no longer exists. If you terminate the manager for some impropriety or possibly theft, you may decide not to offer severance at all.

Severance Package Techniques And Standards

- Pay the manager maximum of two weeks severance pay for every year of employment.

- Pay the manager $50 to $100 per day for every day early that they vacate the apartment.

- Offer to allow the manager the use of a storage space for up to 60 days, unless they are being terminated for theft.

- Offer to extend health insurance benefits for up to 60 days. This is most commonly done through COBRA.

Remember: When terminating an employee, it is best to conjure up your courage and get it over with! Always ask someone to act as your witness and to accompany you to the firing. Try to fire the employee early in the week. And if possible, conduct the meeting away from the facility.

When you meet with an employee that you are terminating, be candid and very clear about what is occurring. Explain to the employee that there is no longer a fit between the employee and the company. Protect the self-esteem of the individual. Remember that you probably made a poor hiring decision. Some employees are so devastated by a firing that you might consider asking them if they want to "voluntarily resign."

Be sensitive. In most instances, the employee will initially be devastated by this event. Realize that you are hitting them cold and allow them to vent their feelings. Assure them that the decision is not personal. Try saying something like this: "You are a good person. You have done some good things here, but I no longer feel as though this job is right for you. I think you will be happier somewhere else." Above all, never change your mind once you commit to terminating a manager. They may cry, scream, or beg, but do not waiver.

It is a good idea to use a termination checklist that includes the following:

- The manager needs to remove all personal property from the office immediately.
- Immediately change the locks and explain to the employee that this action is to protect both parties.
- Reconcile the petty cash and any outstanding deposits in transit.
- Ask the manager to disclose any/all units that they are currently using.
- Ask the manager for all keys to overlocks, closets, carts, etc.
- Ask the manager for the password to the computer software, if appropriate.
- Have the manager's name removed from the calling list with the alarm company.
- On a no-fault termination, agree on a "cover story" that will be used when others inquire. For example, it is very common for customers to ask about what happened to the previous manager. The cover story is the explanation that will be given to parties who ask about the managerial change. For example, a common cover story to use is "John and Betty decided to move closer to their grandchildren." The cover story, assuming that the owner/property manager consent to it, allows the departing manager to save face in the event they see their vendors, fellow managers, and customers again.
- Assure the exiting managers that their names will not be disparaged in any way by succeeding managers or other company personnel. Additionally, brief the incoming management team that the previous managers cannot be discussed with anyone and to use the agreed upon cover story.
- Be sure to remove the manager's code from the gate system.

Terminate managers as though they were your parents. Be gentle, compassionate, and help them save face.

Use the following phrase: "You are a good person. You have done some good things here, but I no longer feel as though this job is right for you. I think you will be happier somewhere else.

Tips For De-Hiring Managers

• Terminate managers as though they were your parents. Be gentle, compassionate, and help them save face.

• Use the following phrase: "You are a good person. You have done some good things here, but I no longer feel as though this job is right for you. I think you will be happier somewhere else."

Prevention Strategies

There are several things that you can do to protect yourself from legal and operational problems when terminating poor performers. Practice the golden rule. Fire as you would like to be fired. Next, have a written employment agreement, with specific provisions regarding occupancy, with all employees and never deviate from getting it signed and properly executed before allowing anyone to work or occupy the apartment.

Always choose to err on the side of fairness and compassion. Oftentimes judgment can become clouded due to personality clashes. While you feel as though a manager is not deserving of anything, the reality is that in most instances you made a hiring decision based on desperation rather than qualification. Spend a few extra dollars to make the transition smooth and amicable.

When hiring, use some of the many personnel tools available on the market. Credit checks are a good place to start. Make it clear that credit is just one of the background checks and that one's credit record is not dispositive in hiring. After all, good credit is usually a good sign of a responsible individual. When conducting credit checks, you may discover that a candidate has poor credit. If this is true, discuss the issue with the potential candidate. In many instances, the manager may have suffered a traumatic health problem or family crisis that destroyed their credit. Bankruptcies, while generally viewed as a negative component in hiring, may have a plausible explanation.

Be sure to ask the prospective candidate if it is permissible to conduct a credit check on them. Sometimes their response can be very revealing. You can purchase software from your local credit bureau and conduct credit checks for less than five dollars per inquiry, but you must have written permission to conduct a credit check. You can also cross reference addresses on the credit report with self-storage addresses.

Background checks are also important; they have become critical in self-storage management. Considering the fact that security is such an integral part of self-storage, I am surprised that more property managers/owners do not make this a part of their routine procedures. The background check can be very revealing and should always be done. There are many companies on the Internet that perform this service or provide this information. In many cases, you do not even have to actually conduct the test if you mention it in the exploratory interview. For example, a common phrase is: "Before I hire a manager, I conduct a criminal background check. Is there anything you would want to tell me before I conduct the check?" It is amazing what many applicants will confess with just that one question being asked. The companies performing such investigations will usually provide the necessary releases and disclosure forms to do this correctly.

Drug tests are occasionally used in the self-storage industry. There are usually several drug testing labs in most metropolitan and even rural areas. These labs can be found in the *Yellow Pages* under "Drug Detection & Testing." Generally, drug testing will cost between $50 and $100 per applicant.

There are literally thousands of employee tests out there that cover many areas of aptitude. Normally, in self-storage we are interested in math, problem solving, and sales skills. In many instances, self-storage property managers/owners will also use general intelligence tests. The Internet is a great resource for employee testing. Remember that your testing criteria must be pertinent and applicable to their actual job duties.

CHAPTER TWO

Staffing For Dollars And Sense

There are three things in life that a person takes seriously: their dog, their kids, and their money—in that order! Consequently, when it comes to hiring new managers, compensation can be a very sticky subject. Obviously, a new candidate will want as much as they can get. Surprisingly enough, however, many self-storage managers actually rate money as number three or four on their list of job motivators.

Most managers want a few specific things from their employer. First is job autonomy. Most storage managers want to feel as though they can make decisions and manage the property. If you are hiring on-site managers, the apartment or living quarters are very important. After all, this is where they spend the majority of their time. If you build a larger apartment with amenities, you will attract better managers. Health insurance and benefits are also important. Due to the "graying" population from which we tend to hire, health insurance is more important than you might think. And of course, money is always important to everyone. Think of it this way: If you were to purchase a $2 million dollar Learjet, would you hire a minimum wage pilot to fly it?

Negotiating Compensation

So how do you determine the right income and benefit package? Ask around at conventions or meetings to find out what the going rates are for self-storage managers in your area. Try to determine what the job is worth in today's market. Most property managers/owners are ignorant to current wage levels. Determine how much you can afford to pay a manager based on the economics of the facility. Remember that minimum wage laws typically apply, whether or not the facility can afford them. This is especially true for small facilities.

Don't be afraid to pay well for good, talented managers. In the overall scheme of things, another $500 to $1,000 per month is cheap for motivated people. Also, if you choose to hire a person or a team away from another facility, you should pay approximately 10 percent more than their current salary. If the previous employer does not offer benefits, this may represent at least a 10 percent increase in compensation.

In addition, be sure to consider a benefits package. In today's self-storage industry, most managers want and expect benefits and a bonus program. It is a good idea to structure a bonus program so that approximately 70 percent of their compensation is fixed and 30 percent is tied to performance.

Common Manager Benefits In The Self-Storage Industry

Health insurance—Don't cheap out on health insurance. A poor health insurance program will diminish motivation more so than no health insurance at all. Therefore, buy the best health insurance money can buy.

Lodging with utilities paid in full—Cable television is always an issue with self-storage managers who live on site. Think about buying a satellite receiver if standard cable is not an option.

Two to three weeks paid vacation—Storage managers cherish their time off. You should offer at least two weeks of paid vacation per year and require the managers to take it. Also, encourage your managers to take three-day weekends to maintain their sanity.

Five to 10 paid sick days per year—Since storage managers deal directly with the public, they need a sick day policy. In most cases, since two individuals work in the office, this is not a big problem. When hiring individuals, sick days are important.

Insurance coverage on the apartment contents—Most standard insurance packages typically cover the manager's apartment and its contents. Check for this coverage and be sure to tell the manager about it.

401K savings plans—In the past, 401K plans were only found in larger companies. Today, you can set one up through your self-storage association.

Monthly bonuses as agreed upon by the property manager/owner. For bonus programs to be effective they must be simple—a good bonus program is one that enables managers to calculate their bonuses within five minutes after the end of month close. In addition, bonus programs need to be tailored to the needs of each individual facility.

Longevity bonuses given to managers who stay with the employer—Some property managers/owners have had luck with longevity bonuses. Longevity bonuses reward the manager for staying at the facility. This is very effective with facilities in "economically-challenged" neighborhoods.

Staffing Considerations

There are several key wage and hour issues you need to consider, depending on how you configure your facilities. Currently, there is a debate and a trend toward non-resident managers versus the tried and true resident manager concept. Here is the debate and some relevant personnel issues:

Resident Managers

The resident manager concept has been an integral part of the self-storage business since its infancy. The original theory behind hiring resident managers was that they provided on-site security and the employer provided lodging, which was an attractive part of their compensation. The resident manager concept is slowly changing. Many owners/operators are abandoning the resident manager concept.

Arguments For Resident Managers—They provide necessary security and theft deterrence. The resident manager approach involves no travel to the employment location. The managers take a proprietary interest in the facility since it is also their home. Most banks/lenders prefer this configuration. Customers perceive this as being more secure and convenient.

Arguments Against Resident Managers—Most thefts will occur, in spite of having resident managers; therefore, does this approach really deter crime? Managers are difficult to handle when the employment relationship ends. Resident managers tend to "burn out" after two and a half years. On-site, resident managers can project an unprofessional, "mom and pop" image to the customer. Resident managers, unless supervised properly, are more prone to embezzle. You limit your possible candidates by requiring a couple or team. Overtime hours can bury you. It's easier for a resident manager to allege thousands of hours of overtime.

Non-Resident Staffing
In the self-storage industry today, non-resident staffing is becoming more common place. The non-resident staff member does not live on the property and leads a more "normal" life. The non-resident staffing concept is gaining popularity for many reasons.

Arguments For Non-Resident Staffing—Non-resident employees lead a "normal" life and come to work more refreshed. Non-resident employees have a longer "burn-out" period. Non-resident employees are easier to terminate when things do not work out. Any individual becomes a potential management candidate. A more professional atmosphere is created when the employee does not live on the facility. You do not incur the additional mortgage and construction cost of building an expensive apartment.

Arguments against non-resident staffing—The payroll cost is higher with non-resident staffing. Customers assume that all facilities have on-site resident managers. Your competitors could capitalize on this fact. Self-storage thieves look for resident managers. You may be more vulnerable to theft. The apartment can be a tax-free benefit to the employee. A non-resident manager may not have the same proprietary interest in the property.

Determining The Right Compensation
Compensation levels for self-storage managers have climbed. The Fair Labor Standards Act dictates certain minimum wage levels. In states

Cost Considerations

If you offer an apartment for your on-site managers, you will incur certain specific costs. Typical costs include:

- Utilities like gas, electric, and water/sewer (approximately $100 to $300 per month)

- Additional debt service for the cost of the apartment. The apartment is the most costly building on the property (approximately $300 to $600 per month in additional debt)

- Maintenance costs (i.e., carpet cleaning, appliance repair, pest control, etc.)

- Fair market value of apartment must be included when calculating Workman's Compensation premiums (approximately $50 to $100 per month)

A non-resident or remote configuration would not incur any of these costs.

where the state law exceeds the FLSA, the state minimum must be used. For example, the minimum wage in New York is greater than the federal minimum. There are some guidelines to consider in terms of employee compensation.

Full-Time Resident Managers
- Resident manager team salary range: $1,800 to $4,500 per month
- Apartment and utilities are included: $100 to $300 per month
- Use of one storage space is typical: $75 to $150 per month
- Health coverage (optional): $550 to $1,375 for two employees

Remember, regardless of "combined" salary, most states require hourly wage designation and the keeping of time records. Therefore, it is incumbent to keep accurate time cards showing all hours worked by all employees.

Most resident managers want and now expect a bonus program. The best bonus program is the one that motivates the managers. A good rule of thumb is that the manager should be able to calculate his or her bonus five minutes after the end of month close. Structure the bonus program so that it represents 20 to 30 percent of the employee's total cash compensation.

Examples Of Cash Compensation/Bonuses

- Percentage of the gross revenues: one to five percent
- Per unit bonus: $2 to $10 per rental
- Per unit bonus on net rentals (move-in minus move-outs): $2 to $10 per unit
- Percentage of revenue over a base amount: five percent of revenues over $50,000
- Mystery shopping bonus (based on minimum score): $50 to $500 per month
- Commission (packing/moving supplies, truck rental, etc.): percentage of sales

Full-Time, Non-Resident Managers
Facility Manager, average salary: $12 to $20 per hour
Health coverage (optional): $200 to $700 for one employee
Bonus: See suggestions above

Part-Time, Non-Resident Managers
Assistant manager: $9 to $12 per hour
Bonus: See suggestions above

Note: Most facilities should operate seven days a week. Therefore, a part-time employee is needed.

Maintenance Personnel
More facilities are now hiring full- or part-time maintenance personnel. They typically earn $9 to $12 per hour.

Wage And Hour Considerations
Self-storage is plagued with several misconceptions regarding wage and hour regulations. Here are three common myths about wage and hour regulations:

Myth #1: I can pay my manager a salary and work them as many hours as I like.
Truth: Self-storage managers typically do not meet the criteria for exempt employees, therefore they must be paid minimum wage and overtime.

Myth #2: Time cards are not necessary because I pay them a salary.
Truth: Self-storage managers must be paid minimum wage and overtime, even if their time is simply "on-duty" time. Your best protection is to have them complete and sign time cards.

Myth #3: I give them an apartment, so I don't have to worry about overtime or minimum wage.
Truth: All states limit the credit that you can use for the "employer-provided lodging" in meeting the minimum wage requirement. For example, most states have a maximum credit in place that can be used to meet the minimum wage requirement. Consult your legal counsel for the latest laws.

Legal Requirements For Self-Storage Managers
To be legal, you must pay your managers for all hours worked. Therefore, a manager must be paid overtime if: they work more than eight hours in a work day; they work more than 40 hours in a work week; or they work seven consecutive days.

While the overtime rate is 1.5 times the calculated hourly rate, in instances where a manager works more than seven consecutive days, they must be paid double time in most states. In almost all cases, you will be subject to the Federal guidelines since at least one of your customers will reside outside of your state.

It is also essential to have a clear understanding of deductions. Housing may be deducted if it is not a condition of employment that the employee lives on site and only a convenience to the employer. You can apply a credit toward meeting the minimum wage requirement for the employer-provided lodging. This credit varies by state, however; in most instances a dollar amount maximum will apply.

In terms of record keeping, you must keep the following employment records on file for three years:

- Name, address, and social security number of every employee.
- Dates of work, days worked, hours worked, and the weekly total.
- Hourly pay rate.
- Commissions or bonuses paid.
- Deductions allowed by law.
- I-9 Immigration and Naturalization Form.
- Federal Withholding Allowance form.

The most common problem arising out of resident manager teams is the hold over of terminated managers in the facility apartment. If a manager digs their heels in, it may take 45 to 90 days to evict them. The risk can be managed with a well-drafted employment agreement. You can avoid problems by remembering the following:

- Never hire a manager without having them first sign an employment agreement with specific language on the residence or a separate agreement on the residence
- Always hire your employees on an "at will" basis.
- Require all employees to submit time cards and always pay them for all hours worked.

- Seek proper legal advice and review when drafting employment documents, handbooks, and policy manuals.

Friendly And Motivated Managers

Remember: Happy managers rent spaces; unhappy managers do not. It is important to pay your employees well, treat them with respect, and challenge them to excel. You must maintain a positive work environment. Remember, properties don't compete, your managers do. Ask yourself, "Would I want this job?" Better yet, "Could I live in that apartment?" Above all, if your managers do not seem to be happy, find out why. It may or may not be within your control, but it is your problem to solve. When polled, managers list the following (in order of importance) as motivating factors they look for in an employer:

- **Job autonomy**—Managers do not want to be property babysitters with no decision-making authority.
- **Living quarters**—A bigger, nicer apartment with some amenities. Would you want to live in their apartment?
- **Health insurance**—Since they come into contact with customers every day, they need good health insurance. Cheap health insurance is worse than no health insurance at all.
- **Money**—Managers are typically underpaid for what they do. If you purchased a three million dollar Learjet, would you hire a minimum wage pilot to fly it?

If you constantly monitor these key areas, you will accomplish 90 percent of your marketing goals. There are literally millions of books written on how to market. Marketing is not something you do; it is something that becomes a part of your life. Marketing is, in essence, everything you do! Many self-storage owners/property managers think that marketing is just the advertising specialty items or the radio advertisements. Marketing is the entire product delivery cycle, from initial phone contact to waiving good bye when the customer departs. Happy managers make marketing easy!

CHAPTER THREE

Once The Manager Is Hired

S tarting your new managers off right is essential. Unfortunately, most owners hire new managers and throw them to the wolves. This happens most often because the owner does not know or understand the details of day-to-day operations. It's a "sink or swim" approach to management that has ruined hundreds or perhaps thousands of self-storage managers. New employees require a great deal of "hands-on" instruction, support, and feedback.

Just like a newborn, the first month of a new manager's employment determines their attitude and success for the rest of their employment lives. If possible, give the new manager a peer mentor to call upon for help and assistance. Spend an inordinate amount of time with new employees in the beginning and slowly taper your contact off. Do not abandon them and then try to remediate problems later.

Start Out Strong

The first day, week, or month of a new job is the "honeymoon." Take advantage of this phenomenon. Set the right tone by working the new manager very hard in the beginning. This will quickly weed out the poor performer. Most owner's and property managers do just the opposite; they let the new manager "get a feel for the job." Push hard, push strong, and set the right tone.

Always give your new managers too much to possibly do. This makes the job challenging and exciting. It also gives you the opportunity to evaluate their ability to select the most important tasks and to report to you those tasks that were deemed low priority. This can become an excellent teaching tool.

Give a lot of feedback in the beginning. For example, new employees might be phone or on-site shopped every week. Openly discuss their performance early in the relationship. New employees are the most open to critique and analysis early on in the relationship.

Find lots of examples of your new managers doing the right things. Discuss your expectations regarding customer service, sales, collections, etc.

Day-To-Day Management Problems

All of the daily management problems are almost too complex to discuss, but let's discuss a few key and common concepts. First, it is important to recognize that many problems are just temporary or are caused by outside events that are not controllable. Learn to identify these and teach the managers how to cope with them. Next, understand that employees do what you do or they do what you tolerate! This is about the truest statement I have ever heard about self-storage management. Next, almost all employee problems in self-storage are the result of two key problems: lack of direction and lack of feedback.

In terms of lack of direction, you must give clear focus and direction. Most property managers/owners think that their facilities can run on autopilot. Even professional pilots must occasionally hand fly the aircraft. The pilot also inputs the flight plan, checks the fuel, contacts the tower, and calculates the weight.

The best investment in time that you can ever make is to train your managers how to think like you do.

Lack of feedback is also important to understand. Many companies have annual or semi-annual performance reviews with their employees. While this is well meaning, the reality is that employees want constructive and honest feedback. The best way to provide meaningful feedback is to teach the manager how to evaluate their own performance. A subsequent chapter in this book outlines financial statistics that can be used to assist a manager in evaluating their financial performance.

Improving Performance

The best way to enhance and maintain good performance is to invest copious amounts of time at the facility. Managers need to know that you care about your investment and about them. Everyone needs coaching and perspective. Virtually all employees want to do a good job. Here are five simple steps for improving your managers' performance:

1. Share your expectations. Most self-storage owners are too vague about their expectations. Rather than saying "I want you to make me as much money as possible," say "I want you to increase total deposits this year by five percent over last year." This is a very specific and measurable expectation.
2. Create a system of self-analysis and regular feedback. It is the most liberating aspect of self-storage management.
3. Never ever assume anything! Always ask the employee to feed their understanding back to you.
4. Remember the three Rs: Reward, Redeem, and Respect. Reward managers for superior performance. If performance is lackluster, allow them to redeem themselves by giving them feedback, encouragement, and coaching on how to meet your expectations. Respect their effort, even if desired results are not reached. There are many factors that affect occupancies, revenues, expenses, etc. If you see that effort is being made, recognize their effort and respect their dedication.
5. What gets measured gets done! When a manager begins to measure any aspect of performance, all employees begin to focus on the behavior. Even professional athletes are curious when their coaches report that they are making 74 percent of all their free throws. Most athletes, armed with this information, will begin to immediately improve that statistic.

Performance Problems
There will always be performance problems in any relationship. The true litmus test of a property manager/owner is his or her ability to solve and address problems effectively. There are, however, a few rules to use in addressing problems. First, always praise loudly in public; criticize quietly in private! Be very specific about performance problems. Give very concrete examples of problem areas. And be a good listener.

Listen carefully and always hear both sides of a conflict before rendering judgment. The mafia, for example, have a process called a "sit down." If two soldiers or underbosses have a conflict, everyone is forbidden from making a rash decision, i.e., "whacking a guy," without permission. The process is designed to slow the process down so that cooler heads can evaluate calmly and render a decision after hearing both sides. In a sit down, the boss will dispassionately listen to both parties and tell each that he will get back to them with his decision. Good managers can learn from this practice.

Tom Says... The best habit you can possibly adopt as a property manager/owner is to always document conversations or to take notes.

Monitor the performance problem area very closely and provide additional feedback if appropriate. When the problem is solved, let the employee know that they have redeemed themselves. And always keep accurate notes and records of all discussions. Try to follow up property visits in writing, clearly defining what tasks you and your managers agreed to do. Most companies only document poor employee performance after it becomes evident that they will probably leave the employment of the company. A common employment-related lawsuit is wrongful termination, and too often storage owners lose these cases. When poor performance is only documented after the relationship sours, it appears as if the termination was retaliatory. It is important to keep good notes, not only on poor performance problems but on good performance as well, the day the employee begins their employment.

Manager Performance Standards

Exactly what are performance standards? And why do we need them? Performance standards are simply ways to measure the desired performance at a self-storage facility. For example, all owners and managers agree that keeping the facility clean is a general performance standard, but agreeing to exactly what needs to be kept clean is specific.

Standards of performance are specific rather than general. When asked "How do you know if you are doing an acceptable job?" most employees respond "Well, I haven't been fired yet." Most owners and managers do not invest time in creating criteria and standards in which managers can use to determine if they are performing successfully. Performance standards can be very general or detailed, but managers prefer to have specific, detailed performance standards.

Performance standards should always establish minimum levels of acceptance. Performance standards can also establish desired levels of acceptance in key areas such as salesmanship, cleanliness, and adherence to safety standards. They should always reflect reasonable expectations. If performance standards are unattainable, unrealistic, or unachievable, they have no value.

It is also a good idea to permit self-evaluation. After all, performance standards allow the manager to evaluate their own performance without oversight of upper-level management.

Who Should Create Performance Standards?
Employee involvement and participation is crucial in setting performance standards. Evaluate the "personality" of the facility and craft performance standards accordingly. For example, some facilities are located in affluent areas where the tenants expect impeccable cleanliness and maintenance. In this type of facility, paint touchup may be a weekly task rather than a yearly task.

Consistency between owner's objectives and manager's objectives must be understood and agreed upon. For example, if an owner has a debt service payment due on the tenth of the month, then collections calls are critically important to the owner.

Every self-storage facility has daily, weekly, monthly, and yearly tasks and performance standards that must be completed. Specific daily, weekly, monthly, and yearly performance standards should be carefully written and reviewed.

Self-Storage Performance Standards
Performance standards can be very detailed if desired. Most facilities that effectively utilize performance standards have very detailed performance standards that are measurable and specific.

First, let's look at delinquent tenant management. It is essential to establish an acceptable delinquency rate at the facility. Most facilities calculate delinquencies using three different calculations (Operational statistics are discussed in a subsequent chapter of this book). Most facilities can operate with no more than 10 percent of total units being delinquent.

Managers must contact delinquent customers by telephone and should be required to document their calls. They must follow the proper procedures. This means all legal notices must be mailed on time. Late fees should be collected pursuant to company policy. Most facilities should establish an acceptable fee waive ratio and closely monitor it.

Salesmanship is essential for today's managers. A good manager should score at least 70 on a phone evaluation. Shop your managers every month for best results. Share the shopping report with all employees and establish a minimum acceptable score. Be sure to send sales literature to every customer possible via U.S. mail or e-mail. Also, ask every customer to purchase supplies, locks, etc. Remember: A good manager will close 90 percent of all on-site customers.

Train your managers properly about security. Lock checks should be performed daily. All paid customers should be overlock free. Vacant units should always be clean and agree with the computer records. And there should never be customer locks on vacant units. In addition, managers should check all fences, beams, cameras, etc., on a regular basis to make sure they are operational.

Training your managers regarding proper auction procedures is essential. They should always make sure that auction-ready spaces are sealed and overlocked according to company policy and guidelines. Advertisements in newspapers should always be correct. Moreover, all auction files are complete.

Train your managers right when it comes to rental agreements. There should be a rental agreement on file for every customer. Each rental agreement must be signed and correct for every customer, with addendums completed on every customer. Also, rental agreements must be properly entered into the computer system and filed correctly.

Daily Duties For Managers

Facility Appeal And Cleanliness

- Office is clean and orderly at all times.

- Public restrooms are clean and well stocked.

- All corridors, hallways, stairwells, etc., are clean and swept. All lifts, elevators, ramps, etc., are clean and swept.

- Aisles, walls, gutters, and roof are free of debris.

- Signs are clean and professional.

- Manager uniforms are clean and neat.

Facility Maintenance

- Parking areas are free of weeds, debris, etc.

- Landscaping is free of weeds, mowed, trimmed, etc.

- Greenery is healthy, neat, and trimmed.

- All lights are operational.

- Unit doors are clean and usable.

- Buildings are free of pests and birds.

- Gutters are clean and in good repair.

- Company equipment is in good working order.

- Preventative maintenance is performed according to schedule.

Specific office procedures should be set up for new managers. This includes keeping computer records up to date, with merchandise professionally displayed. Deposits, administrative fees, and late fees should be collected pursuant to policy. Company forms should also be properly completed pursuant to policy. This includes:

- Cut lock requests
- Automatic credit card authorization
- Weekly reports
- Monthly reports
- Partial payment disclaimers
- Incident reports

Workplace safety should also be established. Make sure that all injuries are reported immediately, all safety devices and guards are intact and operational, and no unauthorized service or repairs are made by untrained personnel.

While these performance standards are in no way exhaustive, they do demonstrate how performance standards should be designed and used. Performance standards also act as a "thinking checklist" for managers. By using a detailed listing of performance standards, all employees can consistently and diligently focus on the proper management and maintenance of the facility.

CHAPTER FOUR

The Importance Of A Training Program

A formal training program sets standards for employees. The best place to teach formal standards is in a comprehensive training program. Training programs also teach employees the company philosophies and values, in addition to policies and procedures. The trainer can confer values by demonstrating them, typically through customer service. Training programs promote efficiency since it is formal, complete, and comprehensive. Most self-storage training programs are not formalized and therefore employees are trained with a "patchwork quilt" of ideas, concepts, and standards. Well-trained employees are better able to handle customers effectively when they have been trained. Employees are less frustrated and generally easier to manage when they are well-trained. The problem is that there is very little published information available on self-storage training.

Training programs come in different forms, each having a different purpose and outcome. Here are the four basic training types that we should use in self-storage:

- **Orientation Training**—Gives the basic knowledge needed to do the job effectively. Orientation training is usually given by an existing employee through on-the-job training methods.
- **Upgrading Knowledge**—Employee has mastered the basics and can use "any time" training activities. These include attending seminars, webinars, reading articles, and other training modalities.
- **Long-term Professional Development**—Training courses for advancement are offered by state storage associations, Inside Self-Storage, and other providers.
- **Resolving Operational Problems**—Training for specific problems or operational deficiencies is usually done by the owner or property manager. Most current training is addressed by providing training on an "ad-hoc" basis when warranted.

In general, training and curriculum development for self-storage managers encompasses four major areas. They are:

- Define how the job should be done.
- Plan the training.
- Present the training.
- Evaluate the training.

Define How The Job Should Be Done

The first step in training is to define how the job you will train others to do should be done. This process involves developing a position analysis. This is an important first step in training. The process needs to be simple, practical, and efficient.

The first step is to develop a list of tasks. The definition of a task is a single element/activity of a job. Jobs are typically composed of several different specific tasks. The task list is comprised of a list of the items that the employees must know and accomplish. This could include, for example:

- Operate the computer correctly for each transaction (daily).
- Attend to the needs of customers (daily).
- Vacuum the carpet (daily).
- Conduct physical inventories (weekly).

The next step is to define the task. This is a description of exactly how a task should be performed.

The second activity to design a position analysis is to design a method to "break down" each task. This breakdown answers the question, "How exactly should a task be performed?" It should tell the how, when, and what of each task and specify any required equipment, supplies, or procedures that are needed. Developing the task breakdown is similar to developing the task list. For example:

- A manager/trainer should think about the preferred way to perform a task.
- Employees who do the work should be observed and consulted.

- Supervisors of those who do similar tasks should be asked to explain how to ideally complete each task.

The task breakdown describes, in sequence, what employees must do in order to perform a task correctly. This should include items such as: How exactly should inventory be taken? What considerations are necessary when conducting the inventory? What types of things will the employee encounter while conducting the inventory?

The third step is to determine the required quality/competency level you expect from the employees; in other words, the consideration of the quality level required for the task. In order to assure these quality standards are met:

- Make sure that the task breakdown will yield output that meets or exceeds quality standards.
- Constantly stress quality as an integral part of each task.

Remember, trainees may not be able to attain required quality levels immediately. Time is needed to build skills necessary to meet quality standards. Employees should be able to identify quality requirements by the time the training is completed and when the desired quality levels need to be met.

Next, you need to prioritize your training. It is important to train according to the importance of the task and/or the order in which that task happens. How would you organize the following?

Tip: Organize based on the importance of the task.

- **Salesmanship**—This task should be addressed first. If the trainer discovers that the employee cannot embrace the selling skills needed, it is pointless to continue the training process. In other words, the employee should be terminated.
- **Computer**—Computer software familiarity is important as it is used every day. The second most important element is using the software.
- **Legal Issues**—New hires do not always immediately encounter legal issues, therefore it is less important in priority. However, it is a good idea to point out "legal red flags" that require an owner's attention.

- Maintenance—Maintenance is important, but less important overall.
- Handling Delinquencies—Delinquent tenant management is critical yet difficult to perform until the previous tasks have been mastered.

Planning The Training

To plan for training, a trainer must first consider the training objectives. After all, you can't plan a program until you first know what the training is to accomplish. Once the objectives have been established, you can develop a training plan that provides a step-by-step written document for others to follow. Within that plan, each training lesson should be planned. Each lesson should:

- Provide a content outline for the session.
- Suggest activities/specific instructions which will help facilitate training.
- Define suggested time to be spent on each segment within the session.

Presenting The Training

Once you are ready to present the materials to the trainees, you can use a variety of training methods to present the material. Lectures and meetings are the traditional approach for training—and they are still effective.

Role-playing is another very effective method of training, especially for sales, marketing, and customer service. On the other hand, when teaching legal issues, contracts, tenant disputes, etc., looking at case studies is an excellent training method. A useful tool for teaching about lien laws, industry history, company procedures, and policies is to utilize self-study materials which the employee can review on their own. When discussing changes in policies and practices, however, conference calls are the preferred method.

Given today's technology, webinars can also be used for training purposes. Webinars are especially good for providing a visual presentation of forms, photographs, legal concepts, etc. Last but not least, on-the-job training is the most popular method used in small organizations. It can be a great method when implemented correctly.

Remember, not everyone is a good trainer. Some of the worst trainers are your current managers!

Training Evaluation

Once the training process is completed, it is essential to get a trainee's opinion of how the training was conducted. Questions you should ask include:

- Did the trainer encourage you to ask questions?
- Did you know who to ask for follow-up help?
- Did you feel good about your training experience?
- Would more or different training be more effective?

Be sure to include this important step in your training program. And be sure to consider the input for future training sessions.

Who Is The Most Effective Trainer?

Few companies are large enough to afford a full-time, professional trainer. The reality is that most training is done by other managers and occasionally performed by property managers. Facility managers make for very good trainers if they have the patience for it and are given support materials. Facility managers are good because they perform the very tasks the trainee needs to learn on a daily basis. On the job training is also effective because the trainee immediately sees concepts in action.

The most effective way to train is through the use of manager trainers coupled with a training outline that he or she follows. Most new managers need seven to 10 days of training to be prepared to operate a self-storage facility effectively. The training manager must display all the characteristics that you want in your new manager. In other words, they must be the role model and, subsequent to the training, the mentor for the new manager.

Lastly, it is a good idea to compensate the training manager in addition to their normal compensation for training managers or assistant managers.

Coaching Or Maintenance Of Behavior

Follow-up is critical! Maintenance of behavior is an educational concept that propounds that the supervisor or manager must invest in the training by knowing the concepts taught and to attempt to maintain the behavior after the initial training. For example, if the training manager teaches the new employee to handle returned checks in a specific way, the owner or property manager must reinforce their training.

When does training stop and supervision begin? The answer is that it never really does. Coaching is the term that we will use for this type of training. Coaching is the ongoing re-enforcement of the positive aspects of the training. It involves:

- Focusing on special problems which must be resolved. For example, all training programs have gaps and holes in the training program. The deficiencies should be addressed and the program changed accordingly.
- Maintaining open and effective communications with employees. Find out if your training program is working. Do the employees learn what they need to know about the job? Encourage their honest feedback.
- Providing employees with ongoing opportunities for professional growth. Examples: telephone shopping, on-site shopping, performance standards, seminars, conventions, webinars, etc.

For training dollars to be best utilized, all parties involved in the day-to-day management of the facilities must become invested in the process and participate in it. Remember that while developing a training program can be time consuming, it tends to pay off in spades once the investment in time is made. This is especially true for companies with more than two facilities and companies that are rapidly growing.

CHAPTER FIVE

The Economics Of Self-Storage

W hen it comes to a self-storage operation, there are many vital signs that owners and managers need to monitor. The occupancy rate of the facility is one of them. It can, however, be an overrated gauge of a facility's performance. Managers tend to be obsessed with it, and owners enamored by it. In truth, it is really dollars deposited that counts— not occupancy. It is also important to remember that occupancy rates can be very misleading, depending on how they are calculated.

Understanding Occupancy Rates

There are two primary yet very different ways to measure occupancy: economic and physical. In general terms, economic occupancy is measured as collected dollars versus potential gross income. It accounts for the loss of income associated with tenants who do not pay or those who pay discounted rates. Physical occupancy, on the other hand, equates to the amount of space that is physically occupied by tenants. This can be measured by the number of occupied units or occupied rentable square feet. While economic occupancy tends to be lower than physical occupancy, in some cases it can be higher due to existing tenants paying higher rates than the current asking rate for prospective tenants.

Physical occupancy rates are calculated in two ways:

Method 1

$$\text{Unit Occupancy Rate} = \frac{\text{Total Units Rented}}{\text{Total Units Available}}$$

This method in calculating occupancy rates can be very misleading. Storage managers tend to calculate the occupancy rate using the method below:

Method 2

$$\text{Square Feet Occupancy Rate} = \frac{\text{Total Square Feet Rented}}{\text{Total Square Feet Available}}$$

There can be variations of 10 to 20 percent between these two methods. The more reliable method is to calculate occupancy by square footage. Most software packages compute occupancy this way.

Calculating Economic Occupancy
In order to calculate economic occupancy, add all forms of actual rent collected at the facility (i.e., past-due, current, and prepaid rent). Divide this number by the gross potential of the facility.

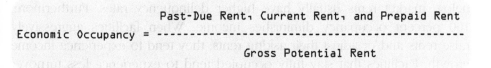

$$\text{Economic Occupancy} = \frac{\text{Past-Due Rent, Current Rent, and Prepaid Rent}}{\text{Gross Potential Rent}}$$

Compare this percentage to the current square foot occupancy rate of the facility. The normal ranges for the variance between these two numbers are one to six points. If there is more than a six point spread between these two numbers, you have a problem. You should suspect:

- Delinquencies
- Prepaid rents
- Possible theft
- Discounts
- Uncollected rents
- Uncollected fees
- Salesmanship
- Rent exceptions

Most good managers can keep this statistic between two to five points, averaging 4.5. This is the most indicative statistic you can track!

The 100 Percent Occupancy Myth

Unfortunately, many self-storage managers and owners will state that 100 percent occupancy is their goal. There are, however, several problems that go hand-in-hand with achieving 100 percent occupancy. First, 100 percent occupancy encourages competition. When self-storage developers are deciding on which markets to enter, they typically cite strong occupancies reported by existing facilities as being their primary indicator of feasibility. Having an occupancy level of 100 percent also erodes salesmanship. If facilities are fully occupied, the employees' selling skills diminish. In addition, 100 percent occupancy gives you nothing to sell. Consumers who contact businesses only to find out that they never have the items they want to purchase begin ignoring the business as a possible purchaser.

Being 100 percent occupied also encourages delinquencies. If a facility is fully occupied, it is typically due to "below market rents;" and facilities with below market rents usually have higher delinquency rates. Furthermore, 100 percent occupancy diminishes income. When facilities aggressively raise rents and/or adjust their asking rents, they tend to experience income growth. Facilities that stay fully occupied tend to experience less turnover since customers stay longer. This does not give the facility the ability to adjust rents to meet increasing demand.

While we will discuss rental rates later in this chapter, it is important to note that 100 percent occupancy has no impact on your ability to raise rents at any time. Many owners believe that rents should not be raised until full occupancy is achieved. This is simply unwarranted since rising costs and inflation will often necessitate a change in rents, just to keep up with rising costs.

Delinquency Rates

Though there are no hard statistics on overall delinquency rates for our industry, there are some good rules of thumb. Delinquencies vary depending on the personality of the facility. Delinquencies also vary from manager to manager. Properties in "economically-challenged" markets have higher than average delinquency rates. There are some common rules of thumb in determining if your delinquencies are within normal ranges.

Almost all software packages calculate delinquency rates differently. How you choose to calculate your delinquency rate is not as important as remaining consistent with your calculations. The sidebar below illustrates three methods for calculating delinquency rates.

Calculating Delinquency Rates

Method 1

$$\text{Lien Delinquency Rate} = \frac{\text{Number of Delinquent Tenants Over 30 Days}}{\text{Total Number of Units Rented}}$$

If this percentage exceeds five percent, your delinquencies are becoming unmanageable and out of tolerance. Most facilities can keep this statistic between two and four percent. These are customers who are in lien status. One of the problems with most software packages is that they consider the customer to be delinquent on their anniversary date. Most customers will pay during the grace period.

There is an indigenous delinquency rate at every facility. The inherent delinquency rate tends to be between 10 to 15 percent of your total gross potential dollars. Another method in determining delinquency rates is by analyzing the total dollars delinquent. The reality is that the manager has little control over the dollars delinquent.

Method 2

$$\text{Dollar Delinquency Rate} = \frac{\text{Total Dollars Delinquent (All Categories)}}{\text{Projected Rent (All Accounts Currently Rented)}}$$

If this statistic exceeds 25 percent, your delinquencies are becoming unmanageable and out of tolerance. Most facilities keep this statistic between 15 to 20 percent. If you notice that the "Method 1" delinquency rate is high, yet the delinquency rate produced by "Method 2" is low, you should suspect that your managers are not enforcing the late-fee policy. The most indicative statistic of theft and embezzlement is a high delinquency rate!

Method 3

$$\text{Unit Delinquency Rate} = \frac{\text{Total Units That Are Delinquent}}{\text{Total Units Rented}}$$

The unit delinquency rate is very simple. It expresses the actual number of customers who are delinquent at any one time. Generally, it should be reviewed at the end of the month. The typical standard for unit delinquency is no more than 10 percent of your customer base should be delinquent at month's end.

Fees Waived

Late fees are an indigenous income stream in self-storage. There is a direct correlation between the number of fees waived and the delinquency rate of the facility. In theory, there should be no fees waived. The reality is that there are many reasons why fees are and should be waived. Below is a good rule of thumb regarding the fee waives.

$$\text{Fee Waived Ratio} = \frac{\text{Fees Waived}}{\text{Total Fees Charged}}$$

The percentage of fees waived should not exceed 10 percent of the fees charged. The industry average for late fees charged is currently $30 due at 30 days of delinquency. Most storage operators charge for each step of the lien sale process. Public Storage currently charges a $10 late fee and a $25 delinquent tenant management fee after 30 days. Late fees act as a deterrent to late payers. Most storage facilities collect three to seven percent in additional income from late fees.

Uncollected Rent And Fees

Every facility will have some uncollected rent and fees. However, you should closely monitor the uncollected rent and fees every month. As you will see in Chapter 9, this is a common way for managers to embezzle monies. High uncollected rents and fees are typically seen in months where the facility conducted an auction. There are no hard and fast rules on how much uncollected rents and fees are acceptable. The best method is to force the managers to document all write-offs to uncollected rents and fees.

Discounts

Every facility has a tendency to offer discounts. The most common self-storage discount is the free month given for a year of prepaid rent. There are not any hard and fast rules of thumb regarding discounts, other than it's generally better to not have discounts at all. A rough and dirty barometer is to divide the discounts given by the projected rent. This statistic should not exceed 8.33 percent.

Rent Exceptions

Rent exceptions are the silent killer in self-storage. Every storage facility has them and they tend to linger with little notice. Most software packages do not show the rent exceptions without a little digging. Rent exceptions seriously affect facility value. For example, if current capitalization rates in your markets are 10.5 to 11 percent and your rent exceptions are only $1,500 per month, this equates to a loss in facility value of $171,428.57!

In theory, it's best to have no rent exceptions. After all, if 50 customers will pay $105 per month for a 10-by-10, why won't all 65 of them? The reality is that customers will tolerate five to seven percent rent increases every year with little or no move-out activity. A good rule of thumb is that your rent exceptions should never exceed five percent of projected rent!

Auction Recovery Ratio

The auction recovery ratio is the amount recovered at the auction versus the total amount of delinquent rent and fees owed by the customer. Expressed as a ratio, this statistic tells us what percentage of delinquent rent and fees are being recovered by the auction process.

$$\text{Auction Recovery Ratio} = \frac{\text{Proceeds From The Auction}}{\text{Total Rent and Fees Owed By All Sold Customers}}$$

Most storage facilities will recover 20 to 40 percent of the total rent and fees owed. The average tends to be 30 percent. If you find that your recovery is less than this average, your managers may be waiting too long before holding auctions. Always have your managers calculate their recovery percentage and encourage them to monitor it closely.

The Question Of Raising Rents

Why do self-storage owners raise rents? The answer varies, but the most common reason is a high occupancy rate. Another common reason is the increasing costs of conducting business; therefore, raising rents is necessary to increase profitability and to recover rising expenses.

When discussing rents, it is important to understand price elasticity. The quantity of space demanded is sensitive to a price change, therefore a storage space is said to be an elastic commodity. Storage rents are said to be elastic for many reasons. For example, homeowners can simply use their garage or purchase a shed for their backyard. There is always the availability of substitutes. Another common reason is the degree of necessity.

If a consumer eventually determines that they are simply storing low-value items, they will become more sensitive to changes in prices. The longer a customer rents, the more sensitive they become to changes in price. Lastly, the greater the competition in a given market, the more sensitive the consumer becomes to price because competitors tend to compete by lowering prices in overheated markets. Hence, self-storage space, like other economic commodities, is elastic and therefore sensitive to changes in price.

Whose rent do we raise? Most facilities raise rents on all tenants. This method is preferred as raising rents on select units begins to create disparity between different size codes. Some owners are reluctant to raise rents on customers who have rented within the last three months and will therefore exclude them from increases. Oddly enough, new renters are less sensitive to rent increases as their satisfaction with storage is still relatively high. Long-standing customers are more sensitive to rent increases and will complain more about them.

When do we raise them? Most facilities raise rents once per year. Many astute owners raise rents during opportune times. For example, in cold climates, the winter months are chosen because vacating would be more difficult. In states such as Arizona, rents are raised when it is hot outside and tenants are more reluctant to leave. Most storage facilities raise rents in April or May, traditionally the beginning of the summer rental season.

How much should space fees be raised? Generally speaking, self-storage customers will tolerate three to seven percent rent increases with little resistance or vacancy loss. This is due in large part to the hassle associated with moving items, securing a truck, paying labor, etc., to vacate over a relatively small rent increase.

Customer Price Sensitivity
Some customers are more price sensitive than others. Large space customers are less sensitive to price increases than small space customers. Business renters are less sensitive to price increases because they can deduct the expense. Credit card customers are less sensitive to price increases because the change in rent is less noticeable. The longer a customer rents, the more sensitive to price they become. Upstairs space renters are less sensitive to rent raises because of the added work to move items into upstairs spaces. These factors should be reviewed when determining rent raise strategies.

Discounting is one way to stimulate rentals. Discounting is good if you tell the customer that their rent will increase at a later date. This is in lieu of giving a customer a discounted rate with expiration. Customers are less sensitive if they know that the rent will increase in advance. Most customers believe that they will vacate the space before the rent escalates, however experience demonstrates that customers tend to stay two or three times longer than originally planned. Discounts can lessen the economic impact to your cash flow; therefore, discounts should be closely analyzed and monitored to be effective.

The giving of free time can also be used to stimulate new rentals. Free time tends to be more effective than lowering the rent rate. The longer a customer rents, the less impact free time has on your cash flow. Customers tend to prefer free time as an incentive to rent. Free time does not affect your rent rate, thereby making any increases seem less significant when annual rent increases are desired.

Your goal is to increase profitability without affecting occupancy. If rent increases are executed every 12 months and do not exceed three to seven percent, few facilities will experience a net loss in income. Most owners are too timid about raising rent rates, both for new renters and especially existing ones. Your income should increase by three to 10 percent every year. The only way to keep up with rising costs and maintain a return on investment is to increase rents. Remember, there's nothing gross about profit!

CHAPTER SIX

The Basics Of Self-Storage Marketing

Marketing is the whole set of activities undertaken to find, influence, and serve customers for products and services. In self-storage, marketing involves five major areas. Without first mastering these five areas, you cannot become effective as a self-storage marketer. In other words, you must focus on the basics first. Thousands of dollars are wasted every year on good marketing ideas because the basics are not taught or mastered.

The Attributes And Location Of The Facility

You cannot change where the facility was built; however, you can enhance its marketability. There are a few statistics and items to ponder. First, most customers live less than 3.3 miles from the self-storage property; they prefer to store at a facility that is close to their home. Next, over 30 percent of all renters will choose you because of your curb appeal. And while visibility is great, poor visibility or location can still be overcome with good telephone skills.

If your facility does have great visibility, you should focus on the several areas. First, utilize flags and banners. Flags and banners are one of the most effective marketing tools, yet we typically fail to take advantage of them. Rotate flags, signs, and banners constantly. Use American flags—it's your right! Use flags of other countries or states. Use a flag with a registered trademark.

Curb appeal is essential. Repaint curbs, fences, etc., constantly. Beautify the facility with landscaping; simple shrubs and flowers can do wonders. Keep the facility immaculately clean at all times. In addition, it is important to monitor the five senses all the time:

- **Sight**—Clean, color-coordinated, sterile surroundings.
- **Sound**—Low, contemporary music in the background.

- **Taste**—Candy bowl, cool water, coffee, and/or soft drinks.
- **Touch**—Cool office in the summer, warm in the winter.
- **Smell**—Clean, pleasing, and fresh.

It is also essential to recognize that the facility golf cart is a sales tool, not a maintenance wagon! Therefore, consider purchasing two golf carts, one for show and one for maintenance. Some managers even display locks for sale on the golf cart.

Security still tends to be the primary concern of most renters. As such, remember that most security measures cost little or no additional money to offer. When looking at the bigger picture, plan to budget constantly for better security at the facility. It will pay off in the long run.

Salesmanship Of The Manager

Your manager determines the success or failure of your facility. It is imperative that they sell well in person and on the telephone. Here are some key points to remember: Approximately 88 percent of all customers call the facility first; only 17 percent of the population has ever used self-storage; and 93 percent of all customers follow up with action.

The best way to increase the salesmanship of your manager is to constantly emphasize the importance of salesmanship, evaluate their performance, and give constructive feedback. This is not always an easy task.

The best way to keep sales performance high is to shop your managers. This can be done by utilizing a mystery shopping service or even a trusted friend to shop your managers. A realistic closing ratio is 50 percent or better. Any manager should be able to score 70 points out of 100 on a shopping test or evaluation. Periodically, have your manager shop their competitors and rate them. They may be surprised! New employees should be shopped more often, not less. Evaluate your managers' sales abilities on site as well.

Customer Service And Conveniences

Today's customers want and expect more conveniences. As such, there are many different types of conveniences you can offer at your self-storage facility.

Accept credit cards: Visa, MasterCard, and American Express. Offer automatic credit card debiting. Customers who pay via credit card stay 40 percent longer. And always buy the equipment—don't lease it.

Sell packing and moving supplies. The best sellers are small, medium, large, extra large, record, and wardrobe boxes. Also, tape, newsprint wrapping paper, and bubble wrap are top sellers. Always mark merchandise up 100 percent. Display your boxes and use banners visible to drive by traffic. Experiment with other items as retail space permits. Accept deliveries. Yes, there is some legal exposure, but it's really minimal. Use a signed disclaimer to protect yourself. Advertise this service everywhere.

Offer monthly billing. Most facilities now charge an extra $1 per month for billing. You can bill all your customers inexpensively with postcards.

Offer a free move-in truck. You can lease and operate a free move-in truck for about $1,200 per month. A free move-in truck is really a great mobile billboard. Good insurance coverage is readily available through most companies.

Extend gate access hours. Longer hours of operation is one of the cheapest, yet most effective marketing tools you have. Most customers cannot access their space until after work. This is why longer access hours are now so popular. Think about the various customer services that you are now providing and brainstorm on ways to enhance or add other services.

Advertising And Promotion
The bulk of all self-storage advertising monies is spent on *Yellow Pages* advertisements. Self-storage ranks number 17 out of 4,200 classifications in the total dollars we spend on *Yellow Pages* advertising. *Yellow Pages* advertising tends to level the playing field. It sources all possible candidates in one area, thereby increasing competitiveness.

While the *Yellow Pages* are used to find our telephone number, a significant percentage of renters actually drive by, are referred by a friend, or are simply repeat customers. Develop a good ad. Hire the services of a professional. Think about air brushed graphics. The best placement tends to be in the first third of the section.

Other types of advertising media can be effective for self-storage, but require a great deal of experimentation. Nevertheless, don't be afraid to experiment with other forms of marketing and advertising. Do, however, make sure you track and document all marketing results when you try other forms of advertising or marketing. This will help you to see which of those methods are successful and which should be dropped.

Internet marketing is now critical to the success of self-storage marketing. Storage renters are using the Internet more and more every day to shop for self-storage. The primary advantage to Internet marketing is that you can show so much more about a facility on a Web site than you can on a two dimensional *Yellow Pages* ad or brochure. In doing so, it's also a good idea to reflect upon what should not be featured on your Web site.

Hire a professional Web designer to create a solid, professional Web site that is interactive and easy to use. While amateur Web designers can create Web sites, a true Web design professional knows and understands what attracts consumers to a Web site and what intrigues them once they visit there. Hire a professional Web designer to create a solid, professional Web site.

There are many Internet sites that promote self-storage facilities. The reality is that most searches will yield good results if your Web site is properly designed and maintained. Most Web designers use other professionals who can maximize your Web site through registrations with several hundred search engines.

Virtually all software vendors now offer integration between their software and your Web site. This gives the customer the ability to "pay online." This feature is beneficial in that it promotes timely payment and reduces the workload on your manager. Ask your software vendor for details.

Planning For Marketing Success

One of the best ways to succeed in marketing your facility is to develop a plan. When things are committed to writing, they have a tendency to get done. Typically, in self-storage we don't even think about marketing until occupancy starts to slip. The reality is that it is usually too late to have any meaningful impact. The best way to approach marketing is to develop a plan and follow it. The sidebar on page 69 offers some tips for developing a marketing plan that is easy to implement and control.

The Key To A Successful Marketing Plan

- Plan your year in advance and commit your plan to writing. When you plan out your year, you have a tendency to think about the seasonal trends. For example, we know that the summer is typically the rental season and that move-outs begin in September or October.

- Conduct your planning during the holidays. Your offices are slower and your managers are typically in a good frame of mind during the Christmas holidays. By having your managers review the previous year's results, they can design a plan that they understand and have a vested interest in.

- Monitor your performance each month. Review your marketing plan every month and make adjustments. Decide what worked and what did not. Remember that a good marketing plan is fluid. If you discover something that seems to work, modify your plan accordingly.

- Give your manager a specific budget to follow. Marketing plans are ineffective if you do not give your managers any money to spend. While the bulk of our advertising dollars are typically in *Yellow Pages* advertising, you should allocate some additional dollars for other forms of marketing.

- Reward your managers for good marketing ideas or efforts. This can be simple praise or recognition. I like to have sales contests every month planned in advance. If you focus more on marketing, your managers will too!

- Lastly, marketing plans need not be complicated; they simply need to be done. A good self-storage marketing plan should appear on one page and should have concrete, achievable goals.

CHAPTER SEVEN

Conducting The Property Visit

While most self-storage owners or third-party property managers realize the necessity of visiting their facilities, many do not plan their visits to facilities. To be effective, you must have an agenda, you must stay focused, and you must leave with a plan for all parties involved. Too many owners/property managers see their role simply as someone who visits the facility to make sure it's still there! To be effective, you must have an agenda.

What should an owner/property manager look for? There's an old adage, "What gets measured, gets done!" Any employee will have a tendency to focus on the areas that you focus on. Therefore, a good property visit should be conducted in a certain order.

Marketing

Marketing is the most important element of our business. Yet, how often do you discuss marketing with your manager? Marketing tends to get pushed to the back burner. For that reason, always discuss marketing and sales at the beginning of your visit. This list should include:

- **Current Specials And Promotions**—What are they and are they working? Do we really need them? What are our competitors doing? Any creative ideas?
- **Flags, Banners, And Literature**—Are they being rotated? Banners and flags need to be rotated every 21 days; over 30 percent of your rental traffic is generated by drive-by visibility.
- **Outside Sales Calls Completed**—Missionary marketing works! If your manager is devoted and believes in it, it will produce results. Were missionary marketing calls made?

- **Incoming Telephone Calls**—Is phone traffic up or down? If rentals are down this month, at least we know why. Daily calls should be logged and tallied.
- **Reasons For Storing**—Why are people renting from us? This question is seldom asked in storage. Our economy tends to run in cycles. Is there a potential opportunity here? Should we react to changing forces in our local economy?
- **Last Telephone Score**—How well did the manager do on their last telephone shop? Was their score up or down? Was their score acceptable?
- **Last On-Site Shopping Report**—How well did the manager score on the last on-site shop? Was their score acceptable? What can we do to improve our selling ability?
- **Uniforms**—Are the managers' uniforms clean, tatter free, and professional? Is it time to order new ones?
- **Ad Sources**—Where are our telephone calls coming from? Is that classified ad working? Are my coupons working? Is my radio station ad working?
- **New Tenant Questionnaires**—What do the new tenant questionnaires say? Are we tracking the statistics? What do these statistics mean? What should we change?

Delinquencies

Delinquencies are an every day part of self-storage. In order to control delinquencies you must be diligent, persistent, and polite. It's easy to become discouraged when attempting to collect delinquent rents. If you sell 20 customers today in an auction, 20 new customers will step into their shoes the next day. To control delinquencies, you must continually urge and coach the managers to never let up. Here are some of the questions you should ask about delinquencies:

- **Review Current Late List**—Are delinquencies too high? Should we bill? Are delinquencies slowly creeping out of control? Are my delinquencies the result of seasonality?
- **Current Delinquency Rate**—Is it high, low, or acceptable? Is the manager working everyday to control delinquencies?
- **Review Files**—Take the time to review the delinquent files on site. Look for notes being taken of phone calls, conversations, etc. Is the manager following up on delinquent accounts?

- **Problem Tenants**—Who are the problem tenants? Are they problems every month? Are there alternatives? Should we evict them?
- **Phone Calls**—Are phone calls being made? Is the manager documenting them?
- **Possible Deals**—Can deals be made with some tenants? Can we motivate them to move out?
- **Inventory Spaces For Sale**—Are spaces ready to inventory for sale?
- **Check Files In Process**—Are lien sale procedures being followed? Receipts? Letters? Newspaper advertisements?
- **Schedule Auction**—When can we schedule the next auction?

Computer Checklist For Store Visits

- **Check Audit File**—Problems? Changes?

- **Run Summary Report**—Problems? Dangerous statistics?

- **Company Units**—Why? Can any be consolidated? Any changes?

- **Reserved Units**—How long? Critical sizes?

- **Damaged Units**—Why? Can they be repaired? Are they empty?

- **Free Units**—Why? Reason?

- **Unavailable Units**—Why? Reason? Are they empty?

- **Check Logons**—Who logged onto the computer? Why?

Store Statistics
You should watch the critical statistics all the time. Too many owners/property managers don't know they have a problem until it's too late.

- **Deposits To Date**—Up or down from previous month? Is this expected?
- **Fees Waived**—Why? Who? How much?
- **Delinquencies**—Acceptable or unacceptable? Growing? Auction time?
- **Uncollected Rent**—Why? Who? How much?
- **Uncollected Fees**—Why? Who? How much?
- **Discounts Given**—Why? Who? How much?
- **Raise Rents On Anyone**—Who? How much? 90 percent rule?
- **Occupancy Plus Or Minus**—Why? Positive or negative trend?
- **Conversions**—Is it time to convert those 5-by-10s?
- **Raise Rates**—Where is the market? Where are we? How long since the last raise?
- **Competition Survey**—Where do we stand? What are our competitors doing? How are we better? Where are we weaker? Any rumors? New ideas?

Maintenance And Cleanliness

Maintenance is critical to keeping a marketable facility. Always walk or drive the property. Note the overall cleanliness of the property. Things to look for are:

- **Store Evaluation**—Excellent or needs improvement?
- **Office Cleanliness**—Clean, organized, and professional? Keep the five senses in mind.
- **Outside Cleanliness**—Clean, professional, well maintained?
- **Cart Cleanliness**—Impeccable or deplorable?
- **Restroom Cleanliness**—Clean, fresh, or similar to a bus station?
- **Halls Clean/Well-Lit**—Clean, lights replaced, open?
- **Asphalt**—Good repair? Cracked? Need maintenance?
- **Painting**—Minor painting needed? Major painting needed?
- **Gutters/Down Spouts**—Clear, open, and running?
- **Gate, Lifts, Elevators**—Operable, maintained, safe?
- **Cameras, Intercoms, And Monitors**—Working?
- **Dumpster Area**—Clean and locked?
- **Landscaping**—Well groomed?
- **Trees And Shrubs**—Trimmed, clean, and orderly?
- **Doors/Latches**—Good working order, secure?

Operations

These are the day-to-day nuts and bolts items. However, they are an important part of the business. Be sure to check them. They are:

- **Rental Agreements**—Randomly select a few new rentals. Are they signed and complete?
- **Policies**—Are they being followed? Is counseling required? Reminders?
- **Security Problems**—Are there any issues to discuss?
- **Complaints**—Were there any received? If so, why? Were they handled correctly?
- **Merchandise**—Is merchandise stocked and priced? Is the inventory accurate?
- **Locks**—Are locks stocked and priced? Is the inventory accurate?
- **Petty cash**—Are there any questionable expenses or concerns? Is the fund large enough?
- **Deposits**—Any delays noticed? Are the policies being followed?
- **Incident Report**—Were there any? How were they handled? Is follow-up needed? If none, why not?

Personnel

We have a tendency to assume that if the employee does not say anything that all is well. The reality is that most employees expect the leader to approach performance issues, bonuses, compensation, etc. Many employees think they will be penalized or judged for making "waves." You, as the leader, must take a leadership role in this area. Make it a part of your routine visit. Questions to ask are:

- **Manager Bonus**—How well did the employee do last month? Does it motivate them?
- **Assistant Manager Performance**—Is their performance acceptable? Can we provide incentives?
- **Sickness, Jury Duty, Vacation**—Any problems or concerns?
- **Job Satisfaction**—Happy? Frustrated? Empowered?
- **Training Needed**—Upcoming seminars? College? Classes? Publications?
- **Performance Review**—Every visit should be a performance review. If exiting employees report that they did not know if they were doing a

good job, you as the leader have failed! Schedule regular performance reviews. Teach the manager how to self-evaluate. Remove bias and favorites. The best manager is the one who performs. After a visit, e-mail your contact compliments, follow up action items, or corrections.

- **Questions?**—Always note the questions they ask. This information helps generate better training material, policies, etc.

Other Issues

Always keep an ongoing project list and review it each month. Goals are magic. You cannot reach your target if you have no idea how to get there. Note projects completed and remove them from the list. And keep open or uncompleted projects on the list, even if they are low priority.

Be sure to keep notes on persistent problems. If you cannot solve a manager's problem due to monetary restraints, simply tell them. Do not allow them to report problems month after month with no definitive answer.

All your property visits should have a definite agenda such as this one. You should always make notes and keep accurate records of your goals and results. If you learn to document and write things down, you will become better at leading and motivating.

CHAPTER EIGHT

Issues For Management Companies

There are several key issues that concern management companies. In addition, these are also areas of concern for owners or general partners who report to investors and charge the partnership a management fee, since in the past several limited partners have challenged the charges and fees assessed by management companies and/or managing partners. Consequently, it is important to understand the common practices and standards in the self-storage industry.

Most management companies charge a management fee of four to six percent of the gross deposited income less offsets such as sales tax, deposits, refunds, or any other liabilities. Fee management companies that specialize in managing properties for others have a tendency to adjust their fee based on competitive bidding against other management companies. Smaller facilities, however, generally pay a higher percentage lower than larger facilities due to their lower gross income levels.

Most management companies charge a monthly minimum fee for management. The typical minimum fee is $1,000 to $1,500 per month or the greater of the agreed upon management fee. Generally, deposits, sales tax, refunds, and returned checks are deducted from the gross income, and the management fee is then assessed on this adjusted number.

Most management companies charge the partnership or owner for out-of-pocket expenses that are over and above the management fee. Commonly assessed charges are:

- Postage and office supplies used to pay bills, issue refunds, etc.
- Copies made for the facility.
- Long-distance phone charges made to vendors, suppliers, etc.
- The prorate portion of advertising design charges, artwork, etc.

In addition, most management companies charge an upfront, "set-up" fee; the typical fee is $1,000 to $5,000. While other charges are not always common, there are several other forms of charges and income for management companies that are reasonable.

For instance, if capital improvements are made, it is not unreasonable to charge a five to 10 percent management fee for overseeing capital improvements. This practice is very common in the apartment and retail shopping center industry.

Additionally, some management companies ask for and get incentives for managing properties. The most common incentive is a bonus of 10 percent of the excess revenues over and above the previous year. Some management companies ask for a split-fee arrangement. The most common example is to be paid four percent of the gross and four percent of the net income. This encourages the management company/partner to keep expenses under control.

You should always have a written management agreement. Most management companies want one- to five-year contracts. Some management companies charge a "franchise fee" for the use of their name if they have built a reputation in a market area. While each management company will have its own policies, there are those that want all employees on their payroll so that a lucrative benefit package can be offered.

A Typical Management Fee Arrangement
The management fee is simply for managing and directing the on-site personnel. This includes training, paying the bills, supervision of the property, conducting auctions, etc. Some of the items that are typically assumed to be included in a management arrangement are:

- Travel expenses of the property manager/owner.
- Office rent, overhead, equipment, etc., of the management company offices.
- Lodging, food, car rental, etc., incurred by the property manager/owner.
- Telephone calls to the facility.
- All payroll expenses associated with accounts payable, receivable, and financial statement preparation.

If you are not assessing a management fee to the partnership, you should. It simply is not fair to all parties involved if the managing party is not compensated for his or her time associated with the day-to-day management of the property. Effectively managing a self-storage facility for a partnership is not only time consuming, but it also involves a great deal of attention. Remember: When it comes time to sell the property, any buyer, appraiser, or bank will impute a reasonable management fee in determining the value and sales price anyway!

Investor And Property Management Reports
There is a popular saying that goes something like this: "Live by the numbers, and the numbers will set you free ..."

One of the most effective techniques for you as an owner or property manager is to discipline yourself to focus on the performance of your properties. When you consciously sit down each month and review the key areas of self-storage performance and commit your results to writing, you will become a more successful owner/property manager. While this process may seem arduous and time consuming, you will find that it will always force you to action.

Why Should I Report To My Owner Or Investors?
Informed owners/investors feel in control. And like it or not, control is one of the most important elements of our lives. Even when things are not going well, at least a feeling of being in control provides comfort. It is also important to understand the mindset of owners and investors. In general, if a facility is not performing, owners typically assumed that there is a management problem!

Here is another very important point to remember: Informed investors will almost always invest with you again in later projects. Investors are reluctant to invest with general partners who cannot explain why things happen, whether good or bad.

It is also essential to remember that this type of reporting will force you to analyze your strengths and weaknesses. By doing so, you will be forced to take action! Also, from an owner's or investor's perspective, bad news is always easier to accept if you have heard about it in advance! Therefore, be sure to report the overall performance of the property, whether good or bad, with a narrative type explanation. Also report trends as compared to previous years or periods.

Keep in mind that when you commit challenges to writing, you are more likely to complete or address them. Plan your reports and understand how they will benefit you. Here are some suggestions:

- Report marketing efforts being made and their effectiveness.
- Report personnel changes, shopping scores, etc.
- Report significant expense deviations.
- Report any event or incident that may have legal implications i.e., employment issues, claims, injuries, etc.

When it comes to management, your best strategy is to under promise and over deliver! What does this mean? Report problem areas, operational changes, etc. Also report current market conditions and why customers are or are not renting. Clients and investors are more understanding when the performance of a property is put into context. For example, if every facility in a given market has a high vacancy rate, clients and investors should hear about it.

More About Reporting

There is an unspoken rule about communication that goes something like this: To over communicate is divine; to under communicate is disaster! That having been said, the most effective method of reporting is to do so on a monthly basis. There are some reports, however, that will only require quarterly reporting.

When reporting to investors or owners, develop a standard format that you can use from month to month. Microsoft Word® has a standard report template to use that allows you to insert graphs, graphics, photographs, etc. And remember, presentation is everything! Professionally package your report, enclosing copies of the computerized reports from the facility.

Bear in mind, the first goal of this type of report is to show that you, the owner or property manager, are doing the thinking. The second goal is to have an informed owner and/or investor!

CHAPTER NINE

Auditing Your Facility

A uditing a self-storage facility is a very important part of the management process. Therefore, we will touch on some of the key issues here. For a better understanding of the auditing process, however, I suggest that you read *Auditing Self Storage, Preventing Employee Theft & Embezzlement,* published by MiniCo Inc., which includes some of the necessary forms and letters used when auditing a self-storage facility.

There are many reasons to audit a self-storage facility, the most common of which is to detect possible theft and embezzlement. Nevertheless, auditing should be a normal part of conducting business in every enterprise. Complete and thorough audits also uncover inefficiencies and mistakes being made every day that expose the facility to grave liability.

While there are many reasons why you should audit your facilities periodically, the four most common reasons are to discover theft and embezzlement, to create an atmosphere of deterrence, to determine compliance with policies and procedures, and to determine compliance with law.

Every business has its own particular vulnerabilities to theft and embezzlement. In fact, a recent FBI crime report states that the losses from internal theft and pilferage far exceed theft from outside sources. For self-storage owners, however, embezzlement can be a recurring problem. The majority of self-storage managers are trustworthy, responsible, reliable, and honest, but embezzlement is often a crime of opportunity. Certainly, cash is the first thought that comes to mind, but cash is not the only asset that may be taken. There are also supplies, equipment, and business and proprietary information that can disappear.

How can the entrepreneur run his or her facility, concentrate on growth, expansion, and an increase in profits, and still maintain a level of integrity in the business to be sure that the assets of the company remain intact? Properly auditing the facility on a routine and consistent basis every year can be a big deterrent.

Creating an atmosphere of deterrence can also be a great preventative measure. Remember: Good people sometimes make mistakes. In difficult financial times, people sometimes do foolish things. When having too many bills and not enough money, one may feel that it is okay to get some assistance from their employer, while their employer does not know about it, fully intending to repay the money before it is discovered missing. Then they find themselves caught, even though they may have had every intention of paying it back.

There are people who purposely set out to gain something by taking what is not theirs by misrepresenting themselves or other circumstances like using someone else's credit cards or checks.

White-collar crime is another name for some types of fraud or embezzlement. You don't need a gun to steal. More money is stolen by white-collar criminals than by bank robbers.

A white-collar criminal is one who uses illegal business practices to take money that doesn't belong to him or her. For example, someone who exchanges goods or services instead of charging a customer rent is a white-collar criminal. But even if it doesn't look like normal stealing, it's just as serious a crime and you can go to jail for just as long a time as a violent criminal.

There are self-storage managers out there who travel from facility to facility and secure employment with the specific intent of stealing until they are caught. The reality is that almost anyone, given the right circumstances, will steal at some point in time during their lives. Therefore, the best way to deter theft is to have internal controls that create an atmosphere of deterrence.

All facilities have policies and procedures that are designed to reduce friction with the customer and to prevent exposure to legal liability. The most honest manager in the world can expose the facility to legal liability that could cost the facility owner thousands of dollars in legal fees, court costs, and restitution.

Policies and procedures are also designed to streamline the flow of information to the owner. Managers who fail to follow procedures increase the work load for everyone involved and corrupt the flow of data.

Another common problem arises when the rental agreements are completed by the on-site personnel. There are dozens of rental agreement problems and errors that are made on self-storage agreements. In some cases, these problems are relatively minor. In other cases, they negate the effect of the agreement entirely. This is another common area of potential legal liability. The only way to evaluate this is to conduct periodic audits.

Determining compliance with the law is essential for any business. The self-storage industry, while simplistic in theory, has many legal pitfalls that can ruin a facility owner. Though most states have very specific and detailed lien sale procedures, few self-storage managers are truly conversant with their state laws regarding lien sales. Since most states have enacted specific self-storage legislation, the managers are expected to comply with these laws exactly. In most cases, a court will impose the doctrine of "strict compliance." In other words, since the lien law is very clearly defined, you are expected to follow the lien law exactly. Failure to mail timely notices by even one day will cause you to lose the case.

There are other laws that must be complied with. For example, most states require the facility to collect sales tax on merchandise. Additionally, most states require that sales tax be collected on auctioned spaces. Once again, the only way to determine compliance is through a complete and thorough audit.

Who Should Audit A Facility?
The auditing function can be performed by virtually anyone. There are distinct advantages and disadvantages to each type of individual chosen to conduct the audit. The most obvious person is the property manager or owner. Here is a brief discussion of each individual who audits the facility:

Property/Area Manager—The property manager is the most probable candidate. The property manager knows the facility, the managers, and the past performance of the property. The property manager also knows and understands the policies and procedures that should be employed each day. Moreover, the property manager is typically familiar with the facility's software package or manual bookkeeping system. The properly trained property manager is perhaps the best candidate for facility auditor. The primary disadvantage to the property manager is that he or she is typically the direct supervisor of the employee. It may be difficult to maintain objectivity when you deal with a self-storage manager on an intimate, daily basis.

Owner—Virtually the same advantages and disadvantages exist between the owner and the property manager. Once again, it may be difficult to wear both hats of motivator and coach, and then shift mental gears to become the objective auditor. However, the properly trained owner is another potential auditor candidate.

Outside Party/Auditor—Most management companies advertise that they provide auditing services. For the most part, management companies are good candidates for thorough and complete audits. Management companies know and understand many of the "tricks" due to their involvement with day-to-day management. Management companies typically charge a set fee for the audit, plus expenses. While their fees may sound expensive, you simply cannot replicate their expertise in auditing and evaluating your facility. Remember: When hiring an outside auditor, be sure to ask whether they are familiar with your software package. It is important that the auditor has a good working knowledge of the software you use. Also, an outside auditor will bring an unbiased and fresh perspective to the audit. Psychologically, it is easier on all parties involved when an outside party audits the facility. Emotionally, it is not the owner or property manager critiquing the facility's policies, procedures, or compliance with these elements.

Accountant/CPAs—Accountants and Certified Public Accountants are highly trained and professional auditors. Accounting professionals will typically review accounting data only; however, their analysis tends to be detail oriented and accurate. Once the accounting professional becomes familiar with self-storage, their proficiency increases dramatically. Accounting professionals also bring a new and totally unbiased perspective to the audit process. The primary disadvantage to utilizing accounting professionals is their lack of expertise in self-storage. Occasionally, accounting professionals can become side tracked by situations they deem "suspicious," while a storage-literate individual would quickly evaluate and understand the problem. For example, it is not uncommon for customers to move into the wrong storage space. The accounting professional would find a space that was vacant in the records, yet occupied by an unidentified renter. This might appear suspicious to the accounting professional. The experienced storage auditor would quickly look to see if there was a space that showed rented but was still vacant in the records. However, when the accounting professionals gain experience in these areas, they become outstanding candidates for self-storage auditors.

Accounting Staff—One of the best candidates for self-storage auditor is the staff accountant. They possess many of the traits of the accounting professional, coupled with an intimate understanding of the facility's performance and managers. Your own accounting staff tends to be inquisitive and typically sees various reports from the facility almost daily. The staff accountant tends to be more emotionally detached than the owner or property manager who interfaces with on-site employees daily. With advanced training, the staff accountant is perhaps the best choice for self-storage auditor. Once again, the primary disadvantage to utilizing staff accountants is their lack of expertise in self-storage. However, this tends to be less of a problem, since they have frequent contact with the day-to-day operations. The best way to bring a staff accountant up to speed is to allow them to work a few days at the facility.

When And Where Should An Audit Be Conducted?

Audits should be routine, but unannounced. The reasons are obvious. When you conduct audits on a routine basis it creates an atmosphere of deterrence. Routine audits also desensitize the on-site employees to the emotional effect of being audited. For example, it is very common for employees to be offended when an audit is conducted for the first time. The most obvious implication in their mind is that the owner does not trust them. Employees who have worked for large corporations know and understand that audits are a routine business practice and are not offended by them. Once audits are conducted on a routine basis the resistance to them is lessened. Remember: Audits should be routine but unannounced in order to be effective.

Let me repeat that: Audits should be unannounced. Never give advance warning about an audit. This undermines the entire philosophy behind conducting audits. The audit is designed to determine compliance with policies and procedures, as well as financial integrity. The best way to judge integrity is to conduct the audit during a normal business day. When employees have advance notice they can hide their misdeeds or destroy evidence.

In order to be effective, vary your auditing times during the year. Don't always audit in April or October. And don't audit multiple facilities at the same time of the year. When the auditor is working, the "grapevine" comes alive. New employees should be audited more frequently; likewise, so should facilities in "economically-challenged" markets. Above all, you should conduct a thorough audit at least once per year.

There are times during the year when theft and embezzlement are more prone to occur. There are situations that make you more vulnerable as well. If possible, the audit should be conducted during these critical times. They are:

- April
- Christmas
- Post Audit
- Personal Problems
- Vacations
- Change in Ownership

April tends to be a vulnerable time due to the pressures of Federal and State Income Tax payments being due. When the Internal Revenue Service pressures a taxpayer to pay past-due taxes, their integrity can be challenged. Since most self-storage managers live on the property, they have few deductible allowances of which to avail themselves. This causes an additional tax liability unless the manager directs their employer to withhold additional taxes. If the employee fails to withhold enough tax during the year, they may owe additional taxes at tax time.

Some managers are tempted during the Christmas season due to the pressures of gift giving. This is also a good time to audit since the activity level is typically slower during December.

One of the most vulnerable times is immediately after an audit. If the auditor has become predictable, the employee assumes that the next audit will be 12 months in coming. Occasionally, you will see theft and embezzlement escalate immediately after an audit.

Personal crisis or turmoil in the manager's life can tempt their honesty. This can range from persistent creditors, DUI convictions, poor health, gambling, etc. Personal crisis can place a great deal of pressure on a manager's finances, especially if dependents are living in the manager's quarters. If your child is in jail and fears for his or her life, almost any parent may become desperate. Anytime you hear of personal turmoil or crisis in a manager's life, you should become more diligent and aware of this tendency.

Just prior to a manager's vacation can be a vulnerable time. In many instances the manager simply "borrows" funds with the intent to "pay it back" when they return. Be aware of this vulnerable time.

When a facility changes hands it can also be a very vulnerable time for theft and embezzlement. The employee typically feels as though they have nothing to lose. They also tend to justify their actions by assuming that the owner does not care about their welfare; therefore, why should they be concerned about the facility? This dangerous attitude can expose the facility to legal problems and erodes the income just prior to closing. Additionally, in many cases the prospective buyer cannot purchase the facility as agreed and the ownership remains intact. Once a manager begins stealing, it's very difficult to stop.

Remember to pay attention to intuition and suspicions. We have a tendency to dispel intuition as illogical and not applicable to a modern business mind. The reverse is actually true. Intuition is simply the result of experience. Experience is the result of bad judgment; and bad judgment is the result of experience. Anytime you have suspicions or feel as though something is not right, conduct an audit.

Where Should I Audit?
This is pretty simple; you should always audit all of your facilities. However, some facilities are more vulnerable than others. Schedules can become

hectic and auditing on a routine basis may be impractical for a variety of reasons. Though routine, a yearly audit is recommended at a minimum; the following types of facilities require a more stringent audit schedule:

- Facilities in "economically-challenged" areas are more prone to theft and embezzlement problems.
- Facilities that cannot be visited on a frequent basis are more theft and embezzlement prone.
- Facilities that use a manual bookkeeping system are vulnerable to theft and embezzlement and should always be audited on a more frequent basis.
- Facilities managed by younger personnel should be audited on a more frequent basis.
- Facilities with very "computer literate" managers tend to be more prone to possible theft and embezzlement problems.

Who Is Most Vulnerable?

The reality is that every facility is vulnerable; however, there does tend to be trends and traits that imply greater vulnerability. Here are eight axioms for theft and embezzlement vulnerability. Do you fit any of these profiles?

1. Absentee owners are the most vulnerable of all. If you cannot visit the facility on a frequent basis, you are more vulnerable.

2. Management that visits the property infrequently. If you do not visit the facility on a routine and frequent basis, you are more vulnerable.

3. Facilities that use a manual bookkeeping system are notoriously inefficient. Manual bookkeeping systems simply do not give very many controls. Facilities that computerize experience an instant increase in income. This increase is not due to theft while using the manual system, but is due to increased efficiency!

4. Facilities that use a computerized system are now more vulnerable to theft than facilities with manual bookkeeping systems. The reason: Owners with manual systems know they are more vulnerable and tend to look more closely at their numbers. Owners with computerized systems believe that the computer solves all their problems.

5. Facilities that are in "economically-challenged" market areas are more vulnerable to theft and embezzlement. Customers in these markets tend to pay more in cash, and the job is more stressful than other storage locations. Additionally, customers in these markets are notorious for not keeping receipts, documents, etc., and will not "rat" anyone out.

6. Inexperienced owners/operators are very vulnerable. New facility owners simply have not had exposure to the problems of day-to-day management. Almost every self-storage owner/property manager has several stories about theft and embezzlement.

7. Non-self-storage association members are more vulnerable to theft and embezzlement. Sounds corny, but it's true. The more involved you are in the day-to-day operations and the rumblings in the industry, the less vulnerable you are to problems.

8. Facilities that sell insurance via the computer are vulnerable to theft problems. This is a relatively new phenomenon in our industry. Some managers have been known to break into customers' spaces that were insured. Why? These customers typically don't complain because their losses are paid!

honesty. Many of these danger signals can be easily explained and may be totally innocent. However, if you see the presence of three or more of these danger signals, you probably have a problem that needs investigating. Here are the most common danger signals:

- Managers who never want to take a vacation.
- Managers who cannot seem to keep assistants or relief managers.
- Discovering that relief personnel are inadequately trained.
- Managers who tell customers that THEY are the owners.
- Changes in the manager's lifestyle.
- Changes in the manager's behavior.
- Managers who never complain!
- Low cash deposits. Most facilities deposit five to 15 percent of their income in cash. Your software can give you accurate data regarding cash, check, and credit card remittances in an instant. You should track this statistic each month and watch for diminishing remittances of cash.
- Delays in making deposits.
- Managers who are too eager to hold auctions. Managers who are "cherry picking" want to sell the space as soon as possible to cover their crime.
- Disorganized offices.
- Suspicions of marital discord.
- Managers who frequent Las Vegas or the dog track.
- Managers with dependents living at the facility.
- Suspicious and unexplainable break-ins.
- Excessively high delinquencies.
- Managers who fail to overlock delinquent tenants.
- Spaces that are overlocked that should not be.
- Managers who do not allow the assistants to contact delinquent tenants.
- Managers who never want to hold auctions.
- Low postage usage, especially if delinquencies are high.
- Suspicious expenditures in petty cash.
- High number of manual receipt books on site or purchased.

Again, you will find extensive information about some of the most common embezzlement techniques and prevention methods in *Auditing Self-Storage,* published by MiniCo, Inc., which is available for purchase at www.ministoragemessenger.com.

CHAPTER TEN

Golden Rules Of Management

The speed of the boss is the speed of the team. Your crew will only paddle as fast as you do. Too many leaders are passive. The reality is that managers crave leadership and want more input and direction. This level of involvement tells the manager that you really do care, not only about them but your own property.

All human creatures crave attention. The best performers get the least amount of attention. This is sad but true. Everyone needs, wants, and longs for significance. Some individuals get significance by pointing a firearm in your face. This gives them significance, power, and control. Others get significance simply by picking up trash along the freeway or running for president. Management tends to focus too much attention on problem solving and too little attention on performance. Effective leaders make a conscious decision to find the things that are going well in addition to the things that need attention.

Schedule "apron time" and learn how life is on the other side of the desk. Managers will think you walk on water if you work behind the counter. This tells managers that you care and that you are willing to "get your hands dirty." It can also be very revealing when you actually labor under your own bureaucracy for a few days. Many owners who invest this time find out just how hard it is to enforce late-fee policies or to explain to an irate customer that the facility is not responsible for theft.

If you measure results, you have a tendency to get them. Even the popular movie "The Secret" speaks to this issue. It almost seems universal that you get more of what you focus on. If you focus on wealth and success, you have a tendency to get it. If you focus on pain, sorrow, and drama, you tend to get even more of it. In managing self-storage facilities, owners/property managers find that when you begin measuring anything, especially results, you tend to get more of them. For example, years ago I began to focus on late-fee waives. I announced to my managers that I was setting a goal of not waiving more than five percent of the fees assessed. Within two months of the announcement, most of my managers were waiving less than two percent of the fees accessed.

You're not running for office, you're running a business. In other words, you have already been elected, you can now start leading. Leaders make the tough decisions. Leaders also know that you cannot make everyone happy all of the time. Many young owners and property managers place too much focus on wanting to be liked; as a result, they refrain from making unpopular yet purposeful decisions. While being loved is nice, your managers want leadership, attention, and direction.

Be willing to share the bucks! Self-storage has traditionally been opposed to paying their employees well. This is due in large part to the rag-tag early beginnings of our industry. Today, the reality is that self-storage facilities are large investments and need the education, skill, and motivation of professional managers. There are now more college graduates managing self-storage facilities than ever before. When a property is performing well, be wiling to share the bucks. If an employee finds a new revenue source, reward him or her for it. If an employee saves the company money by performing repairs or construction that would have otherwise been assigned to an outside source, share a few bucks with them. Remember that it's usually not about money, but rather achievement and recognition—but money is also nice to have!

Make marketing your passion! Focus on salesmanship and marketing all of the time. The reality is that sales and marketing tend to be pushed to the back burner as operational issues tend to dominate the day. Leaders and managers must fight the tendency. Sales and marketing drive demand and keep the properties occupied and viable. By placing focus on sales and marketing, the leader or manager is also telling managers that this is their priority, not replacing ropes on roll-up doors. Every task has its importance, however sales and marketing tend to be forgotten until vacancy rises.

Be ye a doer of the word and not a hearer only! Many owners and property managers attend conventions, seminars, and read magazine articles. While this is admirable, it is a waste of time and effort if ideas are not implemented. Make a habit of keeping a small diary on your person where you can jot down ideas or projects that need to be done. Commit to returning home from a convention and immediately begin putting a new idea into action. Do not make the tragic mistake of having a wonderful insight or stumbling on a good idea while driving and then never implementing it.

Praise in public; criticize in private. This is a simple rule, but not always easy to maintain. Everyone deserves praise as well as critique. Public praise, whether in a display ad in the local paper or at the company Christmas party, is precious to any manager. If criticism is in order, always offer it in private and be sure to take notes. When discussing criticism, always offer two parts praise to one part critique.

Properties don't compete, their managers do! In over 30 years managing self-storage facilities, I have never had a customer say "I chose this facility because it has individual door alarms and cameras. By the way, your manager is a jerk, but the amenities were too good to pass up!" I have managed older, tired facilities with virtually no amenities, as well as brand new, high-tech facilities with every amenity the industry has to offer; in both cases the customers still say, "I chose your facility because you were so nice to me on the telephone. Yeah, those other things were nice too, but I just liked Cindy." Leaders know and understand this important fact; the employees of any enterprise either make you successful or destine you to failure. I have seen highly motivated, customer service oriented managers walk into the worst facilities in the poorest neighborhoods and turn underperforming properties around. Conversely, I have also seen brand new facilities falter because of poor management. If you have an economic winner of a facility, you typically have a winner of a management team.

Never talk about other employees negatively! While it can be intriguing to hear the latest gossip, remember that as a leader or manager, you must always maintain a high level of integrity and never be tempted to talk about other employees. While employees will engage you in these types of conversations, the reality is that they will always suspect that you probably speak poorly about them to others as well.

Constantly think of little ways to reward your employees! It is the little things in life that we enjoy. When you perform some simple deed or reward your manager in a small way, you are showing your manager that he/she is important to you. Leaders and managers tend to get busy and overlook this very important management tool. Managers don't care how much you know until they know how much you care. Many years ago I was talking to one of my male managers about fishing in Florida. Mark stated that he would love to have his own boat for fishing. I assumed that he wanted a fancy, large boat. Mark said, "Tom, I just want a flat bottom John boat that I can easily load and unload and pull behind my car." Then I replied, "Mark, if you and Julie get this facility to 90 percent occupancy by July 1, I'll buy you that boat." Mark stated, "Tom, we really are trying now to fill the facility as fast as possible." I answered, "Yeah, I know, but I want to reward your hard work." On May 16, Mark called my office and exclaimed, "Guess what? You owe me a boat!" Motivation takes many different forms and can arise from some unexpected places. Take the time to get to know your managers, study their wants, desires, hobbies, and dreams. Constantly think of little ways to reward them.

The Theory Of The Red Flag Meeting
The red flag meeting was pioneered by Harold Geneen of AT&T. A red flag simply focuses on the numbers of the enterprise and involves all parties that contribute directly to operations. A red flag meeting encourages honest feedback from all parties, even if the suggestions seem unpopular. This is the time to critically look at operations and financial performance and to create an action plan for the next 30 days.

Here is a simple example of a real life red flag meeting exerpt:

Mel asks, "Our payroll costs seem high, especially compared to last year. Why is that?"

John replies, "We had a lot of overtime due to manager illness and we have been open on Sundays this year where we weren't open on Sundays last year."

Mel inquires, "Do we get much business on Sundays?"

John says, "I think we get some, but frankly I don't really know."

Mel says, "I'll pull out the daily reports for the last six months to see how many rentals we've had on Sundays and give everyone a report at the next meeting."

John summarized by saying, "I don't think the numbers are going to show us that it is even economically justified to stay open on Sundays; I'll be curious to see the numbers."

The red flag meeting concept is designed to get input, to critically analyze decisions, and to get the cooperation of other team members in an organization to commit to follow through so that management can make good, sound decisions.

No question is forbidden or "taboo" in the red flag meeting. All participants must treat each others with respect. Challenging current beliefs and procedures is encouraged and welcomed. Expressed opinions are a must from all participants. If the answer is "I don't know," just say so. There are no sacred cows! There are no interruptions or excuses to leave.

Facility performance is discussed first. This is done by looking at the financial statements for the month, as well as the computer reports generated by the facility. In addition, other ancillary reports such as shopping reports are presented.

- Support staff must report on their functions. For example, the accounting staff would report on any issues.
- New ideas, changes, or projects are "put on the table."
- Prior commitments are reviewed at each meeting.
- 30-day commitments are made at each meeting.
- The meeting is adjourned.

The red flag meeting process is quite simple, yet effective. The meeting format forces everyone to place focus and emphasis on the numbers. Too many businesses wait until things are out of control before action is taken. By having a formal review process each month, it forces all contributing parties to review performance and to commit to specific actions for the next 30 days.

Survival Techniques Of The Successful Self-Storage Owner

Self-storage is a simple business that is difficult to manage. This is due to the myriad of tasks you must monitor, much less ask your manager to do. To be an effective owner or property manager, you must be a leader. People don't care how much you know, until they know how much you care. Here are 10 leadership principles to live by as an owner or property manager responsible for the coaching and leadership of others:

1. Follow The Golden Rule

FACT—The number one motivator cited by storage managers as being important to their job satisfaction is "job autonomy." They don't want to be treated as property babysitters.

Before making decisions that affect your managers, consider how you would want to be treated in the same situation. Don't jump to conclusions. Always hear the manager's side of the story before making a decision. Always involve your managers in decision making.

2. Learn To Live By The Numbers

The numbers do not lie. It's nice to be nice, but we must all strive for results. Even when things are not performing well, it's comforting to sleep at night knowing that everything that can be done is being done. All you can do is all you can do, and in most instances, that's enough. Become disciplined and teach your managers to focus on the numbers.

3. Stand For Truth, Honesty, And The American Way

Self-storage managers are always frustrated by owners or property managers who hide things and do not speak their mind. If the company or facility is in a money bind, tell them! They're big kids, they can handle it. Always be truthful with your managers.

If you do not agree with a request of theirs, tell them. For example, a common manager complaint is that they will ask for something and the owner or property manager will seem to concur and imply that they are "working on it." If your property cannot afford a project, tell them.

You must encourage honesty. If your manager wants a raise, to discuss a delicate issue, or needs to borrow money, encourage them to be honest and tell you their feelings.

4. Become Obsessed With Follow Through
FACT—The number one complaint managers have about their supervisors is poor follow-through skills.

The most common manager complaint about owners and property managers is that they do not follow through. Men (sorry, but it's true) tend to be the worst at follow through. Working for a leader or manager with poor follow-through skills is the pits. It's frustrating, demoralizing, and sets the wrong tone for the relationship. Here are some tips to help:

• Discipline yourself to write everything down that you discuss with your managers. Inexperienced property managers commonly make this mistake.
• Delegate as many tasks as possible. Let's face it: A good leader is a good delegator!
• Keep good files on your visits. Develop your own system for keeping facility files handy and accessible.

5. Be Consistent
Sounds trite, but it is still true. To be effective, you must be consistent. You must always be fair. When you make rules, you must apply them consistently to all employees. This can be difficult sometimes. If you stray from established rules, be prepared to explain why the deviation was made. Consistency is a key attribute of a good owner or property manager. It also limits exposure on employee claims.

6. Let Your Managers Solve Their Own Problems
You could solve their problems quicker than they probably can, but you don't teach problem solving that way. Your job is to provide insight and perspective. You accomplish that by giving suggestions and, ultimately, the desired end result. If the end result is achieved, do you really care how they get there?

7. Always Consider The Cost Versus The Benefit

Don't be pennywise and pound-foolish. It is important to control costs at any storage facility; however, when it comes to labor saving devices, you should purchase anything that will make your manager more efficient.

Teach your manager to be flexible and to think about the long-term impact of decisions. For example, this is why we allow our managers the flexibility of waiving late fees. Is it worth it to lose a $175 a month customer over a $10 late fee? Will a $30 a month postage meter save time away from the facility? Always analyze the cost versus the benefit. In many instances, the benefit is simply better morale and control.

8. Avoid Snap Decisions

This is especially true for personnel decisions. Always hear both sides of a conflict before rendering a decision. Except in extreme emergencies, it is always better to say, "I'll get back to you." Give the manager a reasonable time frame, and then follow through on it. If you make snap decisions, your managers will also. Learn to become disciplined in your decision making. Write down the criteria used in making a decision and investigate all options.

9. Get Another Opinion

FACT—Property management is a lonely and often thankless profession.

As a general rule, those involved in a problem are less than objective when it comes to solving it. In most instances, just defining the problem can be difficult. Once you understand a problem, present it to your spouse, friend, or another owner/property manager. Develop a network of trusted advisors who know your management style. Cultivate relationships with other owners or property managers. In most instances, someone in your group will have experience in dealing with the exact type of problem you are facing.

Always think, gather facts, and establish a plan before you act!

10. Become A Student Of Their Job

FACT—Managers do not respect an owner or property manager who cannot work behind the counter!

In other words, you need to know every aspect of how to manage a self-storage facility on a day-to-day basis. Your managers will respect you more if they know that you can work behind that counter. You may not be as proficient as they are, but they know that you can do it. Would you respect a basketball coach who never played the game?

Remember, self-storage is a simple business that is complicated by the fact that you deal with people.

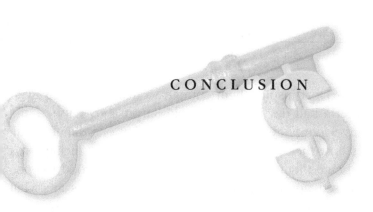

Managing self-storage facilities is an art form. Managing people is a life-long pursuit. Melding the two together is challenging. The problem with self-storage management is that there is very little published information about how to manage self-storage facilities, yet there are volumes of information available on how to manage people. Many self-storage owners and property managers tend to focus on how to manage the property. The reality is that once you have mastered managing the people, the management of the property is easy—it is simply putting the "nuts and bolts" together.

The premise of this book is to encourage you, the self-storage owner/property manager, to identify and choose a management style. The second challenge is to craft a marriage between the "nuts and bolts" of the business and your chosen management style. This involves understanding your management style and then hiring people who can work within it. For example, if your management style is to exercise a great deal of managerial control over your employees, then you should hire employees that need direct supervision. Young managers tend to need constant and direct supervision. Young managers often will work for less and will work hard if encouraged. Younger managers often lack judgment and life experience. Hiring and motivating the younger manager requires more "management time" than the mature employee with years of experience.

Your job as the self-storage owner/property manager is to motivate people! Self-storage is not a particularly rewarding job description. There is no glamour in managing a self-storage facility. While self-storage is a needed service, it is not necessary—like so many other aspects of our economy. The astute self-storage owner/property manager should ask themselves questions like: Why are my employees here? Why are they working for me rather than some other organization? What makes for a good day at a self-storage facility? Do I inspire them enough to make them stay with the organization after a bad day or a bad week? Surprisingly enough, the answer does not involve money. Most people aren't that one-dimensional. Ask the employees how they like their job or the self-storage facility on a regular basis. Encourage them to be honest with you. Be a good listener. Then take action based upon what they tell you. Your values are what make you as a leader or manager of others. If you manage by respecting your manager's values, they will give you 110 percent of their effort.

Too many owners/property managers either delegate too much or too little! You're an owner or property manager because you're good at what you do, but that doesn't mean you're required to do it all or know everything. Your job as a manager is to teach other people how to do a good job or to give them a defined, empirical picture of what a good job looks like. Some owners/property managers are uncomfortable with delegating. One way to overcome this barrier is to start small. Give managers tasks that, if performed incorrectly, can be fixed. Take the opportunity to teach your managers your thinking patterns and empower your employees to make decisions and anticipate trends. Then gradually give them tasks with greater responsibility as you come to understand their strengths and weaknesses. Learn how to anticipate any problems they might have so you can coach them properly before they begin.

Keep your mind open. There is no corner on brains. Even a stopped clock is correct twice every day. Every owner/property manager will espouse that they have "an open-door policy," but the more critical question is: Do you have an open mind policy? Almost every manager in America has an open-door policy, yet few have an open mind about their industry, policies, marketing strategies, etc. Employees are often reluctant to share brilliant ideas because they feel as though their ideas are not significant. A powerful manager will constantly challenge the status quo, ask why things are done a certain way, and encourage their associates to view the business in new and different ways.

Always remind your managers that if they have any questions or concerns, you're ready and willing to listen without bold reaction, anger, or disappointment. Too many parents foil the development of their children by reacting rather than responding. I once had a manager who accidentally disclosed that months prior, our free move-in truck had disappeared for several days. The Highway Patrol was called, the police were looking for the truck, and the manager had sweated bullets for days hoping that the truck would return. The truck finally returned after four agonizing days; the customer had left the truck in the driveway and threw the keys through the mail slot. In further agony, the truck had been driven over 2,000 miles in those panicked days. When I enquired as to why this incident had not been reported to me, the manager said "I was afraid you would be mad at me." It suddenly dawned upon me that perhaps I had not created an atmosphere where mistakes or failures could be confessed without reprisal, judgment, or dire consequences. This incident forced me to reevaluate my range of emotions displayed when confronting unintended events or stupid mistakes that people make.

Don't be one of those managers who inadvertently makes an employee feel like they're "bothering" you when they bring up a question or concern. Always provide a safe vessel for your employees to express their concerns, disappointments, or failures. Instead of seeing it as another crisis to manage, look at it as an opportunity to show your managers how much you want your organization to be a fulfilling place to work. Never minimize or dismiss their concerns, and always make sure that you've answered their questions completely. Remember, a good manager is a good coach.

Let people make mistakes. As an owner or property manager, you will take responsibility for other people's actions, so the last thing you want to do is to contribute to someone else's mistakes. In an attempt to be proactive and prevent as many mistakes as possible, you might give careful instructions and create clear standards and guidelines. This is in fact the "nuts and bolts" of the business. Most managers are afraid of making mistakes, especially ones that might result in litigation. If your managers check with you about every little thing, reluctant to make their own decisions because they might not do it correctly, then you have created the wrong working environment. This makes the manager more dependent on you, which makes them less effective and unnecessarily drains a significant portion of your time. In order for people to think for themselves, they need to learn; in order to learn, sometimes we need to make mistakes. Trust them and give them a fair margin of error.

Learn from your own mistakes and freely admit them. When things don't turn out as expected, recognize what could have been done differently and verbalize this realization to your managers. This shows managers that you make mistakes, too, and it also shows them how they should handle their own mistakes.

Treat everyone fairly and equally, as hard as that might be at times. Most of us aren't as egalitarian as we would like to believe ourselves to be. Many times favoritism happens on a subconscious level. The reality is that owners/property managers will spend a disproportionate amount of time with managers that are performing well, positive, and upbeat. This is a natural tendency and must be recognized to be effective. I once had a husband and wife couple who had worked for the previous property manager and had an exceptional relationship with her. This couple did not like my incursion into the organization and would openly tell other managers about their disdain for me. Finally, the other managers in my organization, during a company meeting, approached me and asked why I had not let this couple go. I explained to my loyal and well meaning managers that this couple had always done an outstanding job and it was for this reason that they were still employed. Finally, I had to approach the disgruntled couple about what I had heard. I explained to the couple that while we did not have a good working relationship, their job performance had been otherwise stellar, but that openly voicing dismay with Tom was creating problems among the ranks. This couple then voiced their anger about how I rarely came to their facility, seldom called, and otherwise ignored them. They felt as though they were treated unfairly and unequally by my absence and that I obviously "disliked them." I explained to them that they had created a situation where they were unapproachable due to their loyalty to my predecessor and that I simply "hated visiting them." I openly admitted that they were not my favorite managers, as a matter of fact, and that I avoided them at all costs. They in turn, admitted that they thought that I was a jerk, but had heard that because they performed well that, that was all that mattered. Oddly enough, we reached an interesting accord; we both admitted fault in establishing and maintaining our relationship and agreed to start anew. This couple went on after their facility was sold and gave me as an interesting reference. They would tell prospective employers that they disliked their previous boss and he disliked them, but that he would give them a glowing reference. I always did because they deserved it!

Being a student of management, I then identified this unusual tendency: We tend to give more positive recognition to the people who remind us of ourselves somehow and who actually like us, rather than to the people who make the biggest contributions to the organization. Upon reflection, I have discovered that it's those people in the latter group who will make the most progress in achieving the organization's goals. A strong owner/ property manager is careful to monitor their own behavior and to make sure that you're not accidentally short-changing them, even if they give you the impression that your positive regard doesn't affect them. I had assumed that my wayward couple was so competent in their knowledge and performance that my recognition as a leader was insignificant. Some people shy away from positive feedback but appreciate it nonetheless.

Managing people is an exercise in disrobing your own ego, prejudices, and preconceptions and, instead, focusing on coaching and cultivating others. Zig Ziglar, well-known motivational speaker and business adviser, said, "People don't care how much you know, until they know how much you care!" Managing the nuts and bolts of self-storage operations is not rocket science, but the careful, deliberate, and compassionate leadership required to inspire others is much harder than rocket science because it involves placing others before one's self. I recently watched a concert by the wonderful and talented singer, Michael Boble who said, "My parents gave me so much love I didn't know what to do with it all." I often think, "Will my son give me a good referral as a parent in 30 years?" I have managed many people over the years and wonder what kind of referral I would receive from them? Am I the type of person that they would want to work with again? Managing and owning self-storage facilities is not about winning a popularity contest, but it is about getting work done with people while maintaining strong customer service, attention to detail, and overall profitability. Think about your approach to managing people and your commitment to becoming the type of leader you would want to follow. This book gives any reader a lot to contemplate. Self-storage facilities are just like children, they flourish when a loving parent gives them a lot of time and attention. Storage facilities flourish when things change, customers are treated like family, and the managers are happy. Storage facilities flourish when owners and property managers chart the course and then let the managers captain the ship. Finally, storage facilities flourish through hard work, commitment, and passion.